IN SICKNESS

AND IN HEALTH

A Love Story

TOM AMLIN

dustjacket

Dust Jacket Press
P.O. Box 721243
Oklahoma City, OK 73172
www.dustjacket.com

Ordering information for print editions:
Quantity sales. Special discounts are available on quantity purchases by corporations, associations, and others. For details, contact the Dust Jacket Press address above.

Individual sales. Dust Jacket Press publications are available through most book-stores. They can also be ordered directly from Dust Jacket; Email: info@dustjacket.com; www.dustjacket.com

Dust Jacket logos are registered trademarks of Dust Jacket Press, Inc.

Cover & Interior Design: D.E. West / ZAQ Designs - Dust Jacket Creative Services

Printed in the United States of America

www.beautifulhandsministries.com
email: beautifulhandsministries@gmail.com

dustjacket

www.dustjacket.com

FOREWORD

I first met Tom and Jackie as a freshman in college. They invited me to have dinner with them in their cottage on the Mount of Praise Campground. We instantly formed a friendship bond. Further, it was obvious to me that they were two people who were madly in love and thus we have this love story book!

Over the years, I was honored to speak at churches where they served and watched and admired the love and concern that they had for one another. I'll never forget the shock and surprise to learn that Jackie had MS. But, as the years unfolded it was easy to see the loving care and the attention to her every need given to her by my friend Tom. Further, Jackie's beautiful spirit, optimistic attitude, radiant face and confident faith made me feel inspired rather than sad and fearful for her.

This book will inspire many people who suffer with debilitating diseases or charged with the watchcase of a loved one. I highly recommend this beautiful love story of two people that I've known most all of my adult life.

Read, weep, rejoice and find resolve to always be at your best in your relationships as well as for the cause of Christ.

– Dr. Stan Toler
Bestselling Author & Speaker
Oklahoma City, Oklahoma

MISSION STATEMENT

I would like for the Holy Spirit to make my introverted personality traits to become strong and extroverted in spreading the Gospel of Jesus. I want to be a good wife, a loving mother, good daughter, and good sister. I always want to be a good example to my daughter and son so they can see Christ is able to meet every need. I want to be a good friend to those around me and when I leave this world I want people to be able to say, "She walked the race, fought a good fight, finished the course, and kept the faith."

– Jackie Amlin

I want to have a humor that can refresh when life seems not to have sunshine and share it in a way that gives hope for the next moment. I want to have His spirit be such a part of me that humor or tears beckon the passerby to seek to know Him. I want to be the husband, father, son, brother, friend that is as pure gold, for I am striving to be without blemish. I want to be able to accept when I am wrong with the right attitude and not boast when I am right. I want to be known as someone others want to be with and can trust; that my word is my bond, and caring is strength. I want it to be said by family and friends, he walked with God and he never let me down.

– Tom Amlin

PREFACE

In the New American Webster Handy College Dictionary, third edition, Webster describes love as 1) A strong affection for another person, esp. of the opposite sex. 2) An object of affection; a sweetheart. 3) Any strong liking or affection." (Signet, 1995) "*In Sickness and Health: A Love Story*" challenges the definition of affection and explores the meaning of commitment and subsequently the precipitating relationship between married couples devoted to the Lord. Do individuals standing before the minister in a beautiful ceremony understand the vow and covenant they make to each other with the words spoken so quickly "in sickness and health"? How do committed couples develop a deep devotion to each other despite tough times? Do couples stay committed throughout the course of the sacred vows exchanged at the altar? How do couples demonstrate their resolve to remain married when disease and sickness wrecks dreams, hopes, and wishes?

This book challenges the definition of affection and explores the meaning of commitment and subsequently the precipitating relationship between a saved and sanctified married couple unquestionably devoted to the full will of the Lord Jesus Christ.

In the subsequent gripping story of a minister and his lovely wife, a clear and resounding theme pervades the text. God is faithful in difficult times. He is able to deliver, yesterday, today and forever – until death shatters the cement of a devoted relationship built upon the foundation of a loving and merciful God. Hebrews 13:8, "Jesus Christ, the same yesterday, and today and forever" provides unequivocal assurance to believers of His inconceivable ability and incomprehensible faithfulness to supply unselfish, gracious, comfort, care and peace, while claiming victory through difficult times.

I challenge you while reading this amazing love story to examine actively and reflectively the vows, covenants and commitments made, and articulated on that exciting and life-changing wedding day, the beginning of life together. Today, do the vows and commitments cement the marriage life? In light of the life-long covenant promised before God and man, consider "Can I trust the God of the universe to meet the needs of my strained and painful reality 'in sickness and in health' – whether emotionally, physically and spiritually?" With Divine inspiration, consider Paul's courageous and obedient behavior while writing his personal epitaph to a close and dear friend, Timothy;

5 But watch thou in all things, endure afflictions, do the work of an evangelist, make full proof of thy ministry. 6 For I am now ready to be offered, and the time of my departure is at hand. 7 I have fought a good fight, I have finished my course, I have kept the faith 8 Henceforth there is laid up for me a crown of righteousness, which the Lord, the righteous judge, shall give me at that day: and not to me only, but unto all them also that love his appearing.
– II Timothy 4: 5 – 8 (KJV)

It is with thoughtful conviction, Divine inspiration, and reflective sincerity the presentation of "In Sickness and Health: A Love Story" begins.

– Dr. Gregory A. McFann,
Ed.D., M.A., M.S.

CHAPTER 1

Yesterday, Now and Then

Jackie and I were just two ordinary people blessed with good friends and a loving family. We have enjoyed the privilege to minister in many parts of this great country. We came from just very simple beginnings, hardworking families that love this country and the people in it. As I sit here writing, I cannot help but reflect on our heritage and where I thought we might be at this time in our lives. Jackie and I knew the value of saving money right from the start of our marriage giving some thought to where we might be, as we entered our later years of life. I've done a good bit of building over the years and always figured in my later days I would build a couple of houses a year to sell. We should be able to live pretty comfortably with the income from the sale of the houses.

I graduated from a great high school located out in the country close to a little town in Champaign County,

Ohio, called Saint Paris. I was blessed with good friends and I have been able to keep in contact with several on a regular basis. I really appreciated my days at Graham High School, even though I could have been a better student. I remember one teacher who tried to get me to study better, and there were times when I guess I did try a little harder. I really liked math, and I guess that was because it was usually pretty easy for me, so with that in mind, I developed the master plan of my life. I knew just what I wanted to do, what I wanted to be, and nothing was going to stop me from success. I would go to college to become a math teacher to supplement what I really desired to do - coach basketball. Great plan that made perfect sense to me, so I decided to ignore, disregard, and run from what I knew God wanted for my life, which was to enter the Ministry. I decided to attend Urbana College, just 13 miles from where I lived and 10 miles from my high school. I decided I would get an education as easily as possible while having a good time, keeping the dream about the beautiful trophies I would win as a great, winning basketball coach. My life in those days was surely not what I should have been doing. I am not proud of my life at that time, and truthfully I was miserable. I had such a tremendous heritage. I knew what was right and yet I ignored it. My mother was a stay-at-home mom who loved her kids, and my father was a hard worker who put his family first while serving God in many capacities. He was first Elder of our home church for many years, taught Sunday School, sang in the choir and quartets, and even with his example, I still would not get serious about changing my goals. I knew I had to stay focused on what I wanted. I guess I was about as good a hypocrite as you could get, and I do regret it. I have heard it said that being saved from that kind of lifestyle gives you a better understanding of life in which you can help others. I say giving your life to Jesus at an early age is better because the baggage is a lot lighter.

For example, my bride of over 46 years, the former Jackie Small, was born at Holzer Hospital in Gallipolis, Ohio to Jack and Vera Small. Jackie's dad came from a large family as had my dad. Jackie's parents were hard workers, and I could not have asked for better in-laws. Jackie was the first grandchild and I can still remember my uneasiness when I first met her extended family. Would they accept me, what would be the outcome? I instantly fell in love with all of them and to my joy, they didn't kick me out.

Jackie and her family moved to Columbus when she was four years old and one of Jackie's aunts invited them to attend church with her at Delray Church of Christ in Christian Union. It was there at the age of eleven that Jackie asked Christ to forgive her of her sins, come into her heart and take control of her life. She regularly attended church, and as a teenager was active in the church youth group. Jackie had a reputation of living a life for Christ at school as well as at church. I remember a mutual friend telling me how she was so respected at Marion Franklin

High School. When Jackie gave her heart to Jesus, she did not keep anything for herself, and it showed.

Jackie was a quiet girl, as well as intelligent. When she graduated, she graduated with honors. She was very good in English, which would be very helpful to her later as a medical transcriber. She was active in drama as well as music in high school. She had a beautiful alto voice, which would also be a blessing later when she and I would sing together. When we met, she was a junior in high school. When we started dating she was going into her senior year so I was able to see her in many of her productions. I was so proud of her. During her senior year, Jackie and her family moved into the Walnut Ridge area so she attended, and graduated from Walnut Ridge High School. Even though Jackie was quiet, very reserved, and the new girl in school, it did not take the music director long to discover her gifts in music and drama. It didn't take the boys longer than the first look to know a new beauty was on campus either. So here we are, two teenagers trying to figure out the next steps in life just like every other teenager. We knew the reality of the uncertainty of life, but we had no reason to think we would be affected by the adversity that others have faced. Did we discuss that topic? No, we were just aligned in our thinking. Things happen to other people.

I now was looking at my wife of nearly 47 years, still lying in her hospital bed in Vancrest of Urbana, but no longer a part of this world. She had just taken her last breath in this health care facility that had been her home for four and a half years. This is really difficult to see her lying there with no earthly life left in her. I am very much aware others have walked this path before me, but this is my day to join the group that didn't ask to be members of that club. The club who now must accept the fate of walking life's road without our partner. This is not our choice. We didn't get to vote. This is not what we anticipated when we decided we wanted to be married.

Jackie had not changed that much since we met. Of course, she looked a little older, but not much. Hardly a wrinkle can be seen, and her hair still lays perfectly in place with just a little "wisdom" gray in it. Because of her natural beauty, Jackie never had to wear much makeup, but once in a while she liked to use a little. I had to learn to help her with her makeup, and for the most part I did pretty well. The aides helped her most of the time after she moved into this care facility. She was still a beautiful girl, and that is not just my prejudiced opinion. Anyone who spent any time with her or listened to her testimony of what Jesus meant to her could recognize she was beautiful inside and out. This disease she battled nearly thirty-three years, Multiple Sclerosis, had taken a toll but even with that, she did not look her age. Her spirit was like a powerful magnet that had no way of letting loose once in its grip. She very seldom complained, and if you asked her how she was doing she would say, "I'm fine." There had been times when the level of pain was so great that most people would have had a difficulty in tolerating it; yet even in those difficult times, she never blamed God. She asked Jesus to take her home, with Him. It was very difficult to watch her go through the day knowing that her day was most always the same. Jackie's spirit would change with a visitor or if she wanted a DVD playing. We played Gospel music most of the time, or the song our son wrote as a tribute to her, entitled "Jackie's Song".

Sometimes on Sunday morning I would go to the nursing facility, and we would have church together. We would have a devotional, pray, and then put on some music or listen to a message. Once we were watching some Gaither videos, and I could tell she was trying to get her hand out from under the covers but she didn't have enough strength. I helped lift the blanket because she wanted to raise her hand in praise to God.

Jackie's day could also include watching some of the old favorite shows, Andy Griffith, the Walton's, to name a couple. She didn't feel like going to the activities very often. With her tremors it was hard for her to play some of the games they had and someone had to help her.

Jackie liked having company. She had more visitors at the health care center than she would have had at home, and she also had some regulars that came once a week to visit.

Jackie had a very nice room, and we tried as much as possible to make it like a room she would have at home. I bought stand-alone shelves, and they were full of pictures, and the cable box for her flat screen TV that her dad had bought her. We installed a DVD player and external speakers so the entertainment system was pretty good. Several shelves were on the wall for more pictures, and a big rug on another wall was a picture of one of our daughter Kelly's horses. There was a big framed poster with pictures of Jackie and me with more pictures under our pictures so she could see them. Every available space on one wall was covered with pictures. I brought a couch, chair, rocking chair, and her special lift chair, so that helped as well. Her room was warm and homey. This health care facility was very impressive and helpful. A few times I would ask them to get her dressed so I could take her in her wheelchair to our house for a little while so she could look around. We would weep over what was and wish for what we could not make happen and then conclude, one of these days we will be perfectly whole.

I am so thankful for the hope we have in Christ. There are things about this life I don't like, but I am at peace to know this is not the end for those of us in Christ.

After a little while she was ready to go back to her room at the care facility. We were able to do that a few times, and then I had to pay for transportation because I could no longer do it safely. We did this as long as possible and then the day came when there were no more trips.

I want to say again that at no time did she blame the Father for not being able to stay at her earthly home.

Sometimes because of her weakened body, she was not able to talk as well as she used to, but she never got to the place where she was not blessed by Jesus. Normally the last thing she wanted to hear at night was the song our son Todd wrote as a tribute to her or the CD from the Toler Brothers.

Prior to her move to Vancrest, Jackie was in the hospital. She stayed in ICU for eight days and then was transported to Vancrest Urbana. I felt she would not be going to our house again but at this point, there was nothing else I could do. For several years Jackie was still at home but I could not leave her alone and of course, there was no way I could afford the cost of hiring help as much as we needed them. We had applied for Jackie's disability and it was granted, so she had been receiving a very small amount of money. Also we had qualified for the waiver program, so we were able to have caretakers come in each day. One of the ladies who helped take care of Jackie bought a DVD of one of the Gaither's homecomings that was recorded in Jerusalem. A song on this DVD, sung by the Hopper's, talks about walking into Jerusalem just like John. Jackie often talked about how she was going to walk into Jerusalem just like John. I think she ran. She talked about seeing Jesus, her personal Savior, and family and friends. She asked me once if I thought our three grandchildren who died before they were born will know who she is. I told her I really believed my dad and mom would be at the front of the crowd welcoming her home surrounded by our grandchildren.

Even up to the end, she still had her sense of humor and the little things she said revealed that sense of humor. Jackie's trust in Christ gave her such hope of something better to come that what she faced here is overshadowed by much promise. Some people that I have visited over the years just want to talk about their ailments and problems, but Jackie wanted to talk about the hope she had in Christ and the promise of a better place where she would be healed.

CHAPTER 2

The Adventure Begins

Let me tell you how God introduced me to this beautiful girl named Jackie Small. I left home one day to attend a youth conference at Circleville Bible College, (now Ohio Christian University) with one thing in mind. I wanted to see some of my friends, have a good time with them and to see a girl that I had started to date. I thought this would make a nice weekend. I did not intend to change colleges or life styles. I was just looking for a weekend of fun. Circleville Bible College hosted what was then called "Youth Conference" each year as a way of ministering to young people as well as to see if they would have an interest in attending the college. This would be the last year I would be eligible to attend because of my age, and I was already attending another college. I hardly got to see my friends who were already students at Circleville Bible College. They lived in one world and I in mine.

I arrived at the college for the youth conference and the girl I thought I was dating was seeing someone else. Talk about an abrupt turnaround. Well, I wasn't real happy about that, and since I really wasn't a Christian, I thought about leaving campus and going downtown to Circleville to see what I could get into. Deep down I knew that wasn't a good idea so I decided I would stick it out on campus. I guess I had at least a little bit of common sense, for a fleeting moment, anyway.

I still wanted to visit with my friends since I did not get to see them very often, and there was not going to be much to do in downtown Circleville. At least at the campus there would be ball games, and other activities. It was not the end of the world, so I stayed. I had already determined some time ago that I was not going to get serious about any girl for a long time. It had only been a short while since a rather serious relationship had ended. I did not want to go through anything like that again, so I figured it was best not getting too close to someone for a long time. Little did I know what this weekend would bring!

I walked into the church for one of the first services and sat down in front of these two girls. I'm not very backward and proceeded to introduce myself. That is when I met Jackie. I knew right away that she was a real nice girl. There was something about her that made her different from most of the other girls I knew. We visited during the weekend but I did not ask her for a date until about a month later. At that point a friend of mine asked me if

I wanted to ask someone to double date with him and his girlfriend. I thought it might be a good idea for me to see if Jackie remembered me. So I took a chance and called Jackie. She was on my mind quite a bit but what would her answer be? I concluded one of the worst things she could say was, "Who did you say you are"? Of course she could refuse to go out with me, too. Her dad answered the telephone and as he went to get her, I could hear him say, "Some guy named Tom is on the phone." I was getting real anxious, , , wondering how this would work, or would this work out at all? I would soon know the answer. This waiting did give me a little time to get prepared for her answer, whichever decision she made. I could not believe how nervous I was. I never experienced this level of anxiety before. I was usually a confident person, but I found myself really concerned about Jackie turning me down, not wanting to go out with me. This thought caused me to be in a greater state of concern than any other time I had asked a girl out. I had dated several girls, but as I have already said, there was something different about this girl.

She answered the phone, and I asked her if she remembered me. She said she did. I then asked if she would like to go out with me. I told her of the plans and she agreed to go. I must admit I was a happy camper and maybe just a little surprised, but most definitely relieved and excited.

I still remember the day we picked Jackie up for our date. As I was walking her to the car, I thought "what a beautiful girl". I could not help thinking to myself as we were driving down the street, "How in the world did I get her to go out with me?" I had dated several pretty girls, but this girl was special. She was perfect in the way she walked, and I could tell very quickly that she was a "lady." Jackie was dressed very nice, but modest, up-to-date, but not at all flashy. Without a word spoken, her humble spirit commanded respect, and the words from her mouth were like that of an angel and her conversation reinforced her spirit.

This recognition of how genuine her spirit was, and of the Spirit of Christ in her life, would be something many people would come to realize was so pure about Jackie.

It did not take long to realize she was quiet, reserved, intelligent and spiritual. I was never quiet or reserved, and I also had not been a Chistian very long. What opposites we were.

We had a great first date. I remember thinking about her and the great time we had as my buddy and I headed home. The thought occupying my mind was could she be the one? Could she be the kind of girl I could get serious about? Would she ever think of going out with me again? Could she be wondering if I was the one for her? This was not the usual date. I had dated some nice girls but this girl was not like anyone I had dated before. I would discover later that God was the reason she was so special and her desire for His will in her life was what made her different. This commitment to Him would put us on a journey for nearly forty-seven years that I describe as a rush I would not have wanted to miss.

I called just a few days later and asked her for another date. I found myself wanting to know more about her. I wanted to know more of her likes, dislikes, interests such as the kind of music and food she enjoyed. I also realized that our goals and interests were the same in many ways, even though our personalities were very much opposite. I was outgoing and Jackie was quiet, more reserved. I also discovered that we both wanted to serve the Lord, which had not been the case until the weekend God made a transformation in my life. Now here I was, dating a girl that I had just met at a life-changing event. I had gone to this conference to visit with some of my friends. Little did I know how much my life would be altered. God certainly had plans for my life that I never had anticipated. Did God make some changes in my life!

Jackie and I both liked music; we liked singing as well as listening to it. We both liked sports, especially the Ohio State Buckeyes. Although this date would only be our second, I could not wait to get there. Just to get to see her, just to be with her, just to hold her hand, to have her close to me!

This would be another "double date" with my cousin and her boyfriend. When we finally got to Jackie's house and she walked to the door, I could see she had cut her hair. It looked so good the way she had it styled. Not a hair out of place. She was afraid that I would not like it. She said most guys like girls to wear their hair long, but I thought it was perfect for her.

Again I was thinking, could this girl be the one for me? Is she the one I would grow old with, share my life with? Have children that would be perfect, with grandchildren that of course would be perfect as well? I could envision us doing things together, helping each other, playing games together. While Jackie and I would never be offered scholarships to play ball, we enjoyed many athletic adventures, such as softball, basketball, ping-pong, and other physical sports. Jackie was not only athletic, she was a beautiful athlete. Could we find ourselves working side by side, taking challenges together, and walking hand in hand through life with not a care in the world? Could Jackie be the one God chose for my helpmate until death do us part? Could Jackie be the one I would share all the things a young man dreams about doing together in marriage until we were old and gray? Did I consider sickness? That thought never entered my mind. I only knew that this could be exactly the girl I had been looking for, and as a result, I never dated another girl after that day. I was hooked better than any trophy fish with an expensive rod. Just the thought of her in my day, every day, made my fragile mind spin.

God became very real to Jackie at age 11. She was a modest, kind, loving person. She was always dressed very modestly. She was very meticulous in the way she cared for her appearance but without a hint of vanity. I think she was an example that a girl, no matter what her age, could be very attractive and modest at the same time. Jackie never wavered in her walk with Christ. The temptations would be there, but the day she fixed her eyes on Jesus, she never took them off. She would always have a popularity of her own but without compromise. Some people live their lives with words like, "I wish I had done," or "if only I had not done," but not Jackie. I can't remember ever hearing her say anything that questioned her decision about giving her life to Christ at an early age. Her walk with Christ was amazing, and the extent of that impact will one day be revealed in heaven.

CHAPTER 3

The Big Day

A year later on June 22, 1968, we both said, "I do," committing our lives to each other, for better, for worse, for richer, for poorer, in sickness and in health, till death do us part. I did not know what it meant to love someone this much. I have to admit, before our wedding day, I was still afraid she would tell me at the last minute that she had changed her mind, but here we are getting married. From the time we started to date until that moment, I considered nothing but how incredible our life would be together. I can't help but wonder when other people make commitments to each other and give vows to each other, what really is going through their minds?

I remember one morning after we were married waking up and looking at Jackie beside me still sleeping and thinking "this is it, Tom". No getting upset over something and deciding to date someone else. I remember thinking "this is it for life". This is a lot more serious than just dating. However, I was OK with that. I had no desire to look elsewhere. I had no problem promising to love, honor, and keep Jackie for the rest of my life. I had no problem promising that I would keep myself only for her. I had no problem with the "have and to hold part", she is beautiful. I had no problem with the "richer or for poorer". We had dated long enough for me to know that Jackie was not a materialistic person and money was not a prerequisite for our marriage.

I had no problem with the, "for better or for worse" part. I really did not know what that meant and did not care. I was a strong healthy guy and she was a strong healthy girl. We would never have to cross the "for worse" bridge. So why should I seriously consider that anything would go wrong? Since I had no problems with the vows as we made them to each other, I could not see any problems in our future. Life was good and this marriage will be great.

We were married for 46 years, 340 days, and we both said we would do it all over again. I know because I asked her. We were blessed many times and yes, we have had some challenges. Our relationship with Christ had grown in ways I had no idea it could be attained. Jackie and I continued to love God even though for over 32 years we had to deal with Multiple Sclerosis, yet Jackie continued to touch many lives. She continued praising the Heavenly

Father, the only living God with her uplifted hands the best she could. She would still tell others how much God meant to her. Wherever Jackie was, she let people know she belonged to Christ.

CHAPTER 4

The Second Most Important Decision I Will Ever Make

Have you ever asked someone how they knew the person they are married to is the right spouse? It was interesting to watch the response of someone when I told them we had been married nearly forty-seven years. Many times they acted shocked, and then they would congratulate us. There was no doubt in my mind that Jackie was the one for me, and she told me even up to the end that she always knew I was the right one for her.

When we talked about marriage, it seemed very comfortable to do. It was just as if we knew God had a plan for our lives. We knew He wanted us together for a purpose. I had no idea our life would find us in so many places, but God had a purpose in directing our paths the way He did. I will share more of that very important part of the story a little later. How would we have reacted if we had known then what we would later face in life together? How would we have reacted in the beginning if we would have known that Jackie would have an incurable illness nearly thirty-three years of our forty-seven years of marriage? I would like to think I would still have wanted to put a ring on her finger. Could I have been confident that God would sustain us "until death do us part" if I had known what Multiple Sclerosis was and what it would do? Could we have developed the relationship that kept us strong during the dark trials of our life if we knew what lay before us? If I had known God planned to use Jackie's illness to minister to others, would it have been enough to sustain our developing relationship? Could we have trusted in Isaiah 41:10? "Fear thou not; for I am with thee: be not dismayed; for I am thy God: I will strengthen thee; yea, I will help thee; yea, I will uphold thee with the right hand of my righteousness." How would we have treated the vow "until death do us part"? I think it is fair to say that it's a good thing God does not show us our futures before they happen. Jackie and I had some challenging moments early in our marriage, like most couples do, without adding what the unknown future would hold.

I can say now, that if I had known then what I know now, I would still want to marry Jackie. This does not make me any kind of Super Saint. It means I would not have wanted to miss any part of this journey together. This life we have had together has been such a blessing in the midst of trials and challenges that I can't imagine, or envision anything else. I would not have picked our script from the menu of life, yet no amount of money or position could buy what I have learned, and the difference I hope it will make in someone else's life after reading this book.

I remember when we went to look at the rings. It was Christmas time, a very special time to begin with, but this year we are starting to plan the rest of our Christmases as a couple. We were starting to plan our whole life together. I only remember one thing; I wanted to get that ring on her finger. I wish I had been more creative, more of a romantic, because I can't remember when I gave her the ring or where we were, but I am sure how I felt when I put it on her finger. It is the same feeling I have today: a love that is hard to explain but made in heaven. I am convinced and confirm to you today, man does not have the capacity to love as I did for Jackie, or till death do us part through chronic illness, without it coming from God.

Jackie and I started our life together when we started dating in June of 1967 and then one year later on June 22, 1968 we made our commitment to live together until death do us part with a beautiful wedding and a good group of our friends and relatives. We were married at the Delray Church of Christ in Christian Union. Jackie was only seventeen and I was just nineteen. We probably should have waited a couple of years, but we were so in love and we just knew that our future together was going to be heavenly. After all, God was the one that brought us together. What could go wrong?

The girls attending Jackie were so beautiful in their matching dresses. The guys of course were very handsome in their white tuxedos, but when Jackie stepped through the door on her father's arm no one could match her beauty. She was just seventeen, two months from turning eighteen, but as I looked at my beautiful bride to be, I knew I was about to marry a Lady. I was watching as perfection walked down the aisle. Her hair was perfect, and she walked with the grace and sophistication of a woman far beyond her years. The gown she was wearing was a perfect fit, but it really would not have mattered what she was wearing at that moment. She could have been wearing one of the burlap bags we used on the farm, and her beauty would have brought it to a level that would make designers of extravagant clothes weep with envy. My mind was saying "if ever I did something right, this was it". I have learned that a smart man marries up, and so that made me a genius. Here we were - beautiful wedding, gorgeous bride, both Christians, great friends and family - about to commit our lives to each other. We have planned our future, and here we go. What could possibly go wrong?

The fall of 1968 would find us living in a little two-room cottage located on our church campgrounds, and we were blessed to have one of the nicer cottages in the area. We had a kitchen that was also a dining room and living room but we had a separate bedroom. The kitchen had a sink, a few cabinets, a refrigerator and enough room left to turn around in, as long as you didn't hit the chair to the dining room set. The dining room set consisted of a table and two chairs. The living room had a heating stove, a couch that opened into a bed, and included the dining room and the dining room set. The bedroom had a nice double bed in it, but it had to be against the one wall so there was room to walk past the bed to get into the bathroom. We did have a back porch where we kept our washer and dryer, but as I said, it was a cottage and we loved it.

I was in my second year at Circleville Bible College, now Ohio Christian University. After my conversion I transferred from Urbana College, now Urbana University. Jackie went to work to help pay our bills. I had a part time job, and with the portion we made on Dad and Mom's farm, we were able to make ends meet. After our cottage experience the first year, the second year we were able to buy a nice mobile home from her aunt and uncle. Jackie and I knew we had to be frugal with our minimal income, and with God's help, we were able to do so and survive. We did not always have what we would like to have, but even then, God would demonstrate His promise and faithfulness to take care of us. We were blessed.

One time we had nothing to eat in the house, which left us with plenty of storage in our kitchen cabinets, and a refrigerator light that had nothing to do. I think we had some mustard and ketchup in the fridge but nothing to use it on. That night when Jackie came home from work, she had with her a box of home canned goods that a friend gave her. She and her husband felt like God encouraged them to share with us. We said "amen, amen," to that as well. While we were blessed several times in our young lives, I believe that was the first time we had faced going hungry. God showed Himself to us by supplying our need. This was only the beginning of the many times God would supply for us, lead us, protect us, forgive us, encourage us, bless us, and the list goes on. It showed us that we were not out of His sight, and that we were important to Him. Satan will use our mind for a playground if we allow it. He does not want us to be able to dwell on the goodness of God because we might get to believing what we read and hear from God. If he can keep our minds on the difficult aspects of life, then it is a distraction to the truth of God. If we are distracted, then thoughts from Satan that God is neglecting us, abandoning us, forgetting our needs can be entertained in our mind. If he can discourage us from hearing and accepting the truth, then we can also come to the place where we believe the lie that we have no value. If we are convinced we have no value, then we might believe we are not worth saving. Our enemy, to whom we are an enemy, does not want us to experience the truth of God which is also the love of God.

CHAPTER 5

Is There Life Without Love?

Love is not the easiest emotion to explain but I know for sure to live through the ordeal that we experienced takes a deeply committed love. I have always felt the scripture gives us the insight to the creator of love. We have a choice what we allow to be the driving force in our lives. I also realize there are people who do not want to accept there is a living God because they are persuaded that God is just the opposite of what He really is. I battled with the nonsense that if I gave my life to Christ, I would not have any friends and there would be nothing to do. Satan is such a liar. When someone tells a lie, how do you know when they are telling the truth? God does not lie and He loves instead of hate. I know that from His word. I know that from experience. The definition of love is said to be:

1. An intense feeling of deep affection.
   "Babies fill parents with intense feelings of love"
   synonyms: deep affection, fondness, tender-
   ness, warmth, intimacy, attachment, endearment;

2. A person or thing that one loves.
   "She was the love of his life"
   synonyms: beloved, loved one, love of one's
   life, dear, dearest, dear one, darling, sweetheart, sweet, angel, honey;

Verb

1. Feel a deep romantic or sexual attachment to (someone). "Do you love me?"
   synonyms: care very much for, feel deep affection
   for, hold very dear, adore, think the world of, be devoted to, dote on, idolize, worship;

   – source unknown

There was something or someway that God revealed
to Jackie and me that we were the right choice for each
other. We had both dated other people, but God was doing something in our lives that would impact many issues
and people.

I can assure you my desire had come to the point that
to serve Father God was the very essence of life. To live
for Christ became a way of life. It was a new thing for me
even though I was raised in a Christian home. To be a good

husband to my wife was the next. We were young and na-ïve to what much of the world was really like, and while a marriage is not always perfect and the parties in it are also sometimes short of perfection, I knew I wanted to give myself to my wife until death do us part. I wanted to try to supply her needs as best I could, give her as many of her wants as I could, protect her from the evil of the world, and always try to keep her beautiful smile on her face. I am blessed to have married a lady committed to the Lord; serving God as a pastor's wife, and a Sunday school teacher. I am blessed to have the joy of singing with Jackie, and to watch her teach our children many important life lessons. Jackie loved her family and liked spending time with them, still she was willing to move from place to place without complaint for ministry. We never know what is down the road until we get there, but one thing we were commit-ted to, "...forgetting those things which are behind and reaching forward to those things which are ahead, we press toward the goal for the prize of the upward call of God in Christ Jesus." Philippians 3:13-14 (NKJV). We knew to have God's best means we must give Him our all. Giving ourselves completely to Him was never discussed because it was never going to be an issue. It was not considered an option. We had one goal for our spiritual lives, and that was whatever He wanted. We wanted God's presence to be a natural part of our lives. As water is necessary for physical life, Christ is essential to our eternal life. There is no reason to discuss something that is not negotiable. This was evident by God's presence being so much a part of Jackie that people could feel and see Him in her life because she would always show and give the best she had while she was able.

CHAPTER 6

The Shell Cracks and Out Comes the Butterfly

Jackie was a person that was very happy just being in the background, doing her thing and no one else really observing or knowing about it. The year we got married, I was still in Bible College and that year I would minister with the drama team. I had been involved with drama and music most all my life starting in grade school as a part of plays and musicals. I continued all the way through school so this ministry in drama would be something I would enjoy. The production was called, COMING READY OR NOT. I was one of the characters in the play, but Jackie was not a student at the college so she could not be in the cast. The director did want her to sing with me so we were blessed getting to do this ministry together. Jackie's choice was for us to sing back stage or somewhere no one could see her and she wouldn't be able to see them.

On one occasion we were to present this play at a local high school. When we got there and began to prepare to set up, she asked me where we had to stand to sing. I told her we had to be on stage. She wanted to know if we could be behind the curtain to sing, and I replied that we had to be a little closer to the front of the stage. Her next question was how close? I really did not want to tell her because I was afraid she would freak out. Finally, I told her we had to be about ten feet from the edge of the front of the stage. Her next concern was how close the students were to us. I really didn't want her to know they would be about two feet from the edge. I thought when I told her we were going to have to call the squad. That may be a little exaggeration but truthfully, she was nervous. To understand how reluctant she was is very important in the beginning of this story. I could never quite understand her nervousness since she had been a part of so many productions, but she was very quiet. Jackie never desired to be the focal point of anything. She was very capable of handling responsibility but never needed the spotlight to feel fulfilled. Our drama team traveled to many churches in several states so naturally Jackie started getting more comfortable being in front of people.

I have noticed that sometimes God puts us in a position where we have no option but to stretch, and to grow. It may not be comfortable; in fact, we may have to face the very issues we fear the most. I do want to assure you, He will not ask us to do something without giving us what we need to accomplish it.

The time in this drama and time in other ministries helped Jackie and by the time we left for our first pastorate, Jackie was more accustomed to being in front of people. She was still quiet but her ability to interact with people, her beautiful personality, her precious spirit, and her love for Christ, was captivating to people. She progressed to the point that she didn't need me to help her when she would speak at a conference without me.

CHAPTER 7
Miracles

Our first church to pastor brought with it some personal challenges and with these challenges would be the time the word "miracle" would be etched into our lives forever.

We loved the people in our church and the community, they were a lot of fun for fellowship. That was a good thing because we had left college, moved four hours away from our family, plus we were expecting our first child. I would need to find a job since the church could not pay us enough to live on. I was young and strong; I had always worked hard and loved challenges so I was not concerned. Keep in mind, God had supplied when we didn't have a thing to eat in the fridge or on the shelf. Our bills were paid and we had no debts, so we had a head start on trusting God for what we could not see.

I had a friend and co-pastor who told me he might be able to help me get a job driving a school bus. That sounded pretty good to me. I started driving a pickup on the farm when I was just a kid, and then of course, I graduated to bigger trucks. I did get my chauffeur's license as soon as I turned eighteen. I had been driving a big truck for a while so I was pretty confident I could drive a school bus. My friend introduced me to the transportation supervisor who then sent me out with one of the mechanics for a test drive. Before I knew it, I was driving a school bus. I liked working with teenagers and kids, so this job made that possible every day. I wasn't much older than a teen myself, but this occupation also brought new challenges that would stretch me and would increase my knowledge of life.

Jackie and I settled into the responsibilities of the church trying to learn how to be a good pastor's family. God was blessing our church and it began to grow as did Jackie with our first-born.

We had a nice parsonage, basic, a little plain but fortunately for us the house was big enough for us to have a nursery. Jackie was a great decorator. She really had a gift for getting the right colors and making them match, plus being able to do something beautiful on a limited budget. Her talent soon had taken a plain house and made it a personal, beautiful, warm home.

It was now time to prepare the nursery so Jackie decided the first thing we needed to do was paint it. In those days we did not know which gender our child would be until birth day, so a color that would work for both is a must. Back then I really did not like to paint. I have since done a lot of painting raising the bar from, "I hate to," to, "I can do it". Jackie had already started to paint and also was expecting me to get in there to help. Being a good husband I entered the room with very low sounding amounts of grumbling. As I tried to walk past the ladder, I bumped into it and spilled paint on the floor. The floor was a nice hardwood, so we had to quickly get it cleaned up. We took care of the accidental mess and started again to cover the walls with this beautiful paint when suddenly I spilled it again! We had another clean up job but this time I was instructed to leave the room. I quickly concluded the last thing a man should do is to argue with a pregnant woman. The best plan of action was for me to leave and as I did, I considered that it only cost me a half gallon of paint to be thrown out. Jackie got the nursery painted, and then I helped with other details of decorating as instructed, all in great anticipation of the arrival of our first child.

While many people talk about the miracle of birth, some miracles are more evident than others. As young couples, I wonder how many really consider the many blessings that we receive, as being blessings, let alone Divine miracles. I do not think Jackie and I were any different, but there is one thing that brought my attention to recognize Divine intervention. The revelation comes with our first child who decided to grace us with her presence on December 5, 1970.

Jackie had not been feeling well for a few days, and of course it was difficult getting comfortable to sleep carrying an extra person around, so sometimes she would try to sleep on the couch. On Friday December 4, Jackie was having a more difficult time than normal. It was about 3:00 a.m. Saturday, December 5 that she called to me from where she was sleeping in the living room to tell me she needed help. I quickly was at her side. Instantly I knew there was a severe problem and we needed to call the doctor. As I look back at it, I should have called the emergency squad but I only had one thing in mind. The doctor's wife, who was a nurse, told me to get her to the hospital as quickly as I could. When we got to the hospital, they examined her right away and then admitted her into a room. All this was standard procedure, but this would not be a "business as usual" situation. The staff was attentive, helpful; just what you would hope you would find in this time of need. But in those days, up-to-date information on each patient was available to anyone. A dry eraser board was placed in the hallway where the names of the expectant mothers were listed along with regular progress reports. It didn't take long for me to figure out how to read their codes, but I wouldn't be allowed in the delivery room; how times have changed.

I remember as Jackie laid there for a couple of hours, and when it seemed like she was stable, I asked her if she felt well enough for me to leave for a little while. I had this routine in the mornings. I would wake up (pretty important first step); I would always get a drink of water and brush my teeth. When Jackie awakened me that morning, I had not taken time to do anything except get her to the hospital. She told me she would be fine. She was finally resting so I left the hospital to head home to brush my teeth, to get my drink of water and to get some much needed cash. In those days if you needed some cash you could write a check at the gas station, and the attendant became your banker, giving you the cash. See, I told you things have changed.

On my way home, I felt very strongly that God was showing me a place He wanted me to pray. I had been carrying a burden for six months for Jackie and the baby. I knew that unless God answered prayer I could lose both Jackie and the baby. That morning as I knelt to pray at the spot God showed me, I remembered something one of my professors had said about one of his experiences. He was also going through a difficult time and yet he told God the situation was in His hands, and however He decided to handle it, he would still serve Him.

God had been so good to us; how could I tell Him any less. I knelt in prayer and told God that whatever He decided to do, I would still serve Him to the best of my ability. I told God that my desire was for Him to bring Jackie and the baby through this situation, but whatever His choice, I would not waiver. I really wanted to instruct God to make it all right, but even in those early days He was helping me to seek His will.

I went back to the hospital and after several more hours, one of the nurses came in to do a routine check on

Jackie and our unborn child. I could see by the expression on her face that something was wrong! She quickly went to get the head nurse. The head nurse was a kind, competent, loving person but definitely the one in charge. She came in and I could tell by the expression on her face, something was wrong. She left the room, went a short distance down the hall to a phone to call the doctor. I got close enough that I could hear her talk, and I heard her say something about the heartbeat. My thoughts immediately went to my conversation with God that morning. I felt this must be the time. Would God answer my prayer in the way that I hoped? Would He give me the blessing of keeping my wife and child living with me here, or would they be going home to heaven? In just a few minutes the doctor was walking down the hallway, all while putting on his white coat, and when our eyes met, he told me, "We are going to operate. We are going for a live baby." I knew instantly everything was going to be fine. I felt the assurance that God was going to let me enjoy my wife and child for a little while longer. Jackie and our baby were going to live. The many hours that we had been there in the hospital waiting! All the stress and anxiety Jackie had gone through! The nine months that Jackie carried our child! The several times they had tried to examine Jackie only to have her hemorrhage! The months of staying before God asking Him to care for my wife and child! He was going to bless us once again!

I went upstairs to wait for Jackie and the doctor to take care of business. I was so confident that God was in the operating room with the doctor that I watched a football game. We guys know how to relax in the face of anxious moments. It was not long until the nurse was at the door to tell me we had a beautiful baby girl. I also wanted to know about Jackie; she assured me she was fine, but that the doctor would be up soon to talk to me. When the doctor got there, he shared with me what the complications had been. He told me that the placenta had separated. If they had waited for our daughter to be born naturally, Kelly would have lost her heartbeat and Jackie would have bled to death. Even if she had been on the operating table, he could not have saved either of their lives. Even then, God was planning something for many years down the road by answering prayer.

In just a few hours both of our parents were there to see their first grandchild, and I was telling my dad about the whole story: how I had carried such a burden for so long. It was then that he shared something with me that he and I had never discussed with anyone until that moment. He told me how he had been carrying the same burden for the same period of time that I had. I have often wondered if there were others who God had given them a burden to pray for us. They may not have known what the details of the need were but they were faithful to pray. I do know the miracle that day was evident. There was no mistaking who made the difference in this story. Yes, I would agree that the birth of a child is a miracle, but truly, that day we experienced a Divine miracle! Was this the end of the miracle? Was there a reason this miracle happened? Was there something God had planned for Jackie and Kelly that was not yet evident? At this point in life we could only see and be happy for the miracle at hand. Jackie and I would grow in our trust in God from these additional answers to prayer, but God was to show Himself in a powerful way as time went on.

CHAPTER 8
God's Plan Continues

After we left the Niles church, we finished another pastor's term at another church before trying to determine what God had for us next. Knowing God's direction means we should follow His leading, but like others have done, I was guilty of second guessing God's will for our lives. I knew God was leading us to go back to Urbana to be a part of my home church, but I resisted that move. I was afraid it was just me wanting to be back home. I had a job offered to me in Urbana, but instead of taking it I went back into the building business in the Columbus area, something I loved doing. We started planning to build a house which would be located an hour from where God wanted us to be. A person would think having run from God's calling for several years I would have learned better!

We pursued a loan to build and yet every appointment we would make with the loan officer at the bank, something would keep that appointment from happening.

Finally, I was able to face the fact that God had a plan for us, and I was keeping us from it. Jackie and I had been living with her parents while we were trying to get a place of our own, so one day when I came home from work, I asked Jackie if she was still willing to go to Urbana if the job offer was still there. She said, "Yes, of course." I confessed to her that what we were trying to do here was not where God wanted us to be, and I was miserable trying to make it happen. I think she knew all the time I was trying to figure out what we should be doing. I called the man that had offered me a job and asked him if the job was still available; he told me to tell him when I could start. I don't think it gets much more open than that. At that time Jackie was carrying our second child, Todd, and within just a few weeks of starting my new job, we purchased our first house. The first night Jackie spent in our new house was when we brought Todd home from the hospital.

God also then opened the door for me to work with the youth at the Urbana Church of Christ in Christian Union and so everything began to fit in place. We had landed, but the big question was, for how long? I had no idea what was yet to come. The blessings, the trials, the tears, the hugs, the beauty, the sunrises, the sunsets, the clear skies, the storm clouds, the joy, the sorrow, the dark nights seemed to turn into lifetimes. We would also face prayers of urgency, have the feeling of aloneness, and the times of comfort when God's assurance would come from His arms wrapped tightly around us. But still we are human so there were questions when the response didn't seem to come when we thought it should. Then blessings came again with answered prayers, victories, and the patience needed to wait for the answer and even sometimes more mountain top experiences. We would experience the reality of the valleys that was needed for there to be mountains, and the pain that goes with growing. We would experience more blessings when God would work through it all to minister to people.

Just a few years later after we had moved twice more, the Lord would give us new direction again. Our District Superintendent wanted us to consider pastoring a church in a little town called Rosewood just three miles from my parents' farm where we now lived. We had purchased a mobile home and put in on the farm. The kids got to experience farm life as well as being next door to two of their grandparents. We really thought this time we could stay settled for a while.

I grew up in that area and knew many of the people there. I worked for some of the farmers in our neighborhood when I was a teen, and I went to grade school in the same little town where the church was located. The church in Rosewood would seem to make sense. It was close to our home; I already had a job, and Jackie had a good job at that point as well. It was a good church with great possibilities, but there was one complication to making that possibility a fact. I did not feel clear that God was directing us to that church. Here is where it starts to really get interesting.

A friend of ours was in Tucson, Arizona during this very time looking at the possibility of going there to pastor a church. He called us to tell us that while he and his wife were there, all they could think about was what a great place it would be for Jackie and me. They had no position of responsibility to make that consideration, but they strongly felt it would be a good fit for us to pastor at that church. I hung up the phone and looked at Jackie and said, "How would you like to go to Tucson, Arizona to pastor a church?" and then laughed. There was no way that could ever happen. God could not be in something like that.

I have never been a person that had trouble with sleeping or keeping an appetite, until then. I could not get this church in Tucson off my mind, and I could hardly sleep or eat. Anyone who knows me may find that hard to accept.

Jackie had even made the statement that if she got behind a truck that said follow me to Tucson, Arizona she would know we were to be there. Here again are the considerations to making this decision. We lived three miles from the Rosewood church, where the kids loved living. We lived next door to my parents, the kid's grandparents, on a farm where we had our own food in the garden and also raised good beef for the freezer. Or, do we travel 2,000 miles from our home to a house we have never seen, a church we have never been to, people which for the most part we do not know, to a part of the country we have never lived and where there is a lot of sand but not a lot of water. To the common sense thinker, this is not a hard decision to make. But sometimes God has another plan in mind. This is when we find out if we really mean it when we say we want God's direction and we will do His will, and yes, we will be what He wants us to be and go where he wants us to go.

There is a song authored by Lynn Keesecker that says, "I'll say yes, Lord, yes to Your will and to Your way. I'll say yes, Lord, yes; I will trust You and obey. When Your spirit speaks to me, with my whole heart I'll agree, and my answer will be yes, Lord, yes."

Sacrifices are not just limited to the people with the action part of God's will. We, as a family of four, Jackie, Kelly, Todd, and me, would do the going, but those staying would be a part of the separation. We would say good-bye to our parents and family, and our parents would say good-bye to their children and grandchildren. What would possess a father to think this is a good idea to once again take his family to another new location, another culture, and an unknown city? To leave a beautiful quiet place in the country, except when the rooster awakens you at dawn? This might be a reason to go. To leave the farming community where you can hear creation start the mornings with a song, and watch hummingbirds drink the sweet nectar from their feeder? To say goodbye to the distinct sound of a baby calf calling for its mother and the lamb bleating as it and the ewe walk with the flock to the pasture field? Why would the family agree to willingly change their lives so drastically just because Dad and Mom feel this is what they must do? Hopefully you will be able to see the answer to this question as you continue reading through this book. This would not be the last time challenges are faced, and neither will this be the most difficult one. You will hopefully see a pattern to God's direction as well as how He helped us with each choice we made.

The 26-foot truck was loaded and behind it was our 1978 Thunderbird hooked for a ride two thousand miles west to Tucson, Arizona.

When I was a kid and we would go on family vacations, Dad always wanted to start early in the morning so we did it just like Dad and started early in the morning. Dad said he and Mom would follow us the three miles to Rosewood just to make sure the car was following all right behind the truck, but I knew there was more to it. He wanted just a few more minutes with his kids before they went a long way off. We had been as diligent as we knew how to be in seeking God's leadership, and He had made it very evident we were to make the trip west to Monte Vista Church of Christ in Christian Union in Tucson, Arizona. God's will does not always make sense to us, and some times in the beginning there is some pain, but His plan always fits perfectly. We left before daylight that morning heading west on a venture that would influence our future in several ways and would forever be a part of our lives. When we got down the road, I had to dry my own eyes. I knew we were doing what we needed to do; we were in God's will, but there were still some questions and pain. This was the biggest trip we had ever taken, especially taking all our possessions with us. Would we like the area? Would the people like us? What would the schools be like for the kids? I knew a family there, but Jackie and the kids didn't know anyone. I had visited there with my parents in 1959, but I was very young then. I didn't remember much.

The trip out was nice. We had as good a time as possible with four people in the single front seat of the U-Haul truck. We enjoyed getting to see parts of this great country that many people only get to read about! I was once again in my comfort zone behind the wheel of a truck. The crowded seat, people trying to sleep, and pulling a big car doesn't bother me. I am comfortable in any size truck but not everyone felt that way. I don't think a lot of thought was given to comfortable ride in 1981 for moving trucks.

In those days there were not as many service stops as there are now. I needed to make sure we had enough gas to get to the next filling station, probably an unknown term to some reading this book. We carried a cooler with things to eat along the way so we picnicked in several states.

It was interesting and beautiful to notice the different terrains we drove through. Some places looked much like what we were leaving and then some were very opposite. To see the different crops raised, large herds of cattle, mountains with their own beauty, and places where you could see the road for miles ahead looking like a ribbon laying in front of you was amazing. Sometimes we would just say,

"Wow." A few times my family would wake up from trying to sleep and ask where we were. In one state the answer went something like this. "We are still in Texas."

We stopped at a Stuckey's in New Mexico to get gas, take a break, and get a pecan log. This place was at a turn in the road out in the middle of a farming community where it was the only shop around for miles. Stuckey's were very unique. They started in 1937 as a roadside convenience store chain. You could find them throughout the U.S. where you could buy candy, novelties, food and fuel.

When we got to Tucson, Arizona, and to the parsonage that would be our home for the next four years, it was amazing what happened. All of our furniture fit perfectly including our freezer. What an awesome God we serve.

We instantly fell in love with the people and the desert. One of the positive moments at the very beginning was renewing friendships. I knew a family that lived there that I didn't get to see much, and now I would also be their pastor.

I remember looking at the beautiful, blue, Arizona sky with not even a cloud the size of a man's hand in it and wondered if I would ever see a cloud again. Would we ever see rain again? Oh, the things that we think of when change comes into our lives.

The house we would live in was owned by the church and it was very nice. It was in a cul-de-sac with a great view of the Catalina Mountains, and God even blessed us with good neighbors. It wasn't but a few minutes after we arrived that there were plenty of people ready to help unload our truck. The long drive from Ohio was successful and what we brought with us traveled well. I was thankful that even the food in our freezer, in the back of the truck, was still frozen. I had placed the freezer in such a way with its cord where I could plug it in at night; plus I wrapped the freezer to insulate it, and it worked. Once again, God was good.

Many times I replay the view of the Catalina Mountains in my mind. I can remember watching the sun as it was beginning to illuminate the landscape. Sometimes the cloud would be at the base of the mountain and then it would rise and descend, as the temperature would change. We could see Mount Lemon right out our picture window, towering over nine thousand feet into the sky with such majesty. Is it possible that God knew we would fall in love with Arizona, or is it possible that when we are willing to blindly follow Him, that He puts a love in our heart so we can be at peace wherever He leads us? Does it matter which it is? I believe it is both. God had never failed us, and in getting to our destination, two thousand miles from home, He still had not failed us. Jackie, the kids, and I would really enjoy our ministry at Monte Vista church. Bless you, Lord.

The beauty of God's creation is not something that can be easily described sometimes. How did God come up with the idea to build such a beautiful structure out of rocks? I was raised on a farm where I rolled big rocks and picked up smaller rocks from the time I knew what a rock was, until I moved off the farm. One of our neighbors in Ohio claimed there is no such thing as a pretty rock and yet there it stood, over nine thousand feet in the air with a ski slope on top of it. One of the most beautiful sights you can find. This rugged and beautiful mountain crying out with more voice than equal of its weight saying, "God made me special."

As we admire His creation, we recognize that what we are able to see is so small compared to the universe. His creation is greater than we can imagine, and everything He designed is special. Even the stars are named, and yet how much more do we mean to Him. We are special, we are His creation and the love He has for us exceeds anything we can see in his creation, as intricate as it may be. He doesn't love only the privileged people. He doesn't love only the people who can perform for Him. He doesn't just love the healthy people, as we will find out. Nevertheless, it wasn't just the beauty of the desert; it wasn't just the beautiful people who made us feel so welcome, and it wasn't how much better I felt physically. It wasn't any of those things that would implant upon our minds something that would last till death do us part. What was it?

CHAPTER 9

Smorgasbord and Dust Devils in the Desert

Jackie was walking through the house one night without turning on the light. We had night lights in our house and street lights that would shine in through the windows, but still she walked into a wall. Naturally, lovingly, I would tease her about walking into a wall. Jackie understood my type of humor and most of the time enjoyed it, but that night humor was cut short. Something was different. There was seriousness about what happened that kept me from saying what would have otherwise been very natural and expected. We did somewhat pass it off and yet there was a noticeable, slight change in Jackie. We had no idea what was happening. We didn't know what to look for so we waited. There was not enough of a change in Jackie to talk to a doctor and what would we tell him, she walked into a wall and she is acting strange? We just pressed on watching for something that might give us some idea of what was going on.

In June, we would have our first Church Youth Camp in Peoria Arizona, at the Southwest Indian School in the Phoenix area. It was a great place to have all of our Arizona churches come together. June was normally just prior to the time of year the monsoons started. It was pretty warm but the nights could get cool and sometimes cold for Arizona. This being our first year to have a youth camp, we were all excited. We did not have an abundance of workers so everyone pulled double and triple duty. Most all of the workers had either attended youth camps or worked in them. Those who had not been a part of either one were very coachable so the unity was excellent. We planned all the activities from classes, chapels, meals, free time, crafts, to sports. I really looked forward to our ball games. Jackie and I would be able to be a part of this together and our kids would be campers so that was exciting, too. It was at a softball game where the campers played the staff that we would begin to face a part of our life that would shape the lives of more people than we could possibly know. It would be a continuation of God's plan for us, even though it would be some time before we would have some understanding of the blessings that can come packaged in pain. It would be the beginning of challenges that would test much of what we thought we knew, and yet would teach us what we had no idea was possible to understand. Life as we knew it would begin to change today at a softball game where the campers played the staff. A time where Jackie was being her normal athletic self, hitting the ball and running. She hit the ball and started to race to first base but about half way there she fell. When the next person got a hit and she started to run to second, she fell again. This was not normal. Jackie was what I would call an undiscovered athlete. She was very good and loved sports. This time she would leave the softball field by me carrying her to her room. She of course had a mixture of embarrassment and a scraped knee. I went back later to check on her, and we still could not figure out what had happened. We decided she should just rest for a while and we would see how she felt after that. The rest of our time at camp was normal except for the nagging question, what happened to Jackie? The sad reality is that would be the last ball game Jackie would ever play.

To some, not playing another softball game is not that devastating. To Jackie it was never a big problem but at thirty-two years old, having been athletic and enjoying playing the game of softball, it can be quite an adjustment in your life. The events that would begin to take place after the conclusion of camp would only be the beginning of challenges.

A few weeks after camp was over, we had to go back to Phoenix for a business conference that took place on a weekend. We were excited to get a little time away; we had been able to reserve a very nice motel. We had never stayed in a two-room suite so we were looking forward to the conference and quiet time. On Friday night, Jackie did not feel like going with me so she told me to go on without her.

I called to check on her, and then when the conference was over that night, I went back to our suite to find Jackie was still not feeling good. The next morning did not give us any better news; she still did not feel good, and the way she felt was different from what we had ever experienced before. I thought maybe we should go home, but she wanted me to go to the conference anyway. I called to check on her mid-morning, and she informed me she was not doing well. I told some of the people that were with us that I was leaving to take Jackie home. I went back to the motel, loaded our clothes, got Jackie, and we headed to Tucson. On our way, we were to pick up our friend Kenny that was going to Tucson with us. When Jackie and I got to his apartment at the Southwest Indian School, Jackie could hardly walk. I helped her into his apartment with many questions on my mind. This was something I had never seen happen to Jackie or anyone else. We soon were on our two-hour drive to Tucson not knowing that the events that we would face that night would be burned into our minds forever. When we arrived in Tucson, I immediately called the doctor. Kenny had to help me get Jackie into the house because she now had no use of her left side. The doctor told me to bring her to the office. What a Saturday evening this would be. This would be a night where I would feel like my whole world was coming crashing down on me. It was to be a Saturday night that I would have no answers for what our world would be like from that day forward, even until death do us part. It would be a night of great emotional pain that

I would never forget. We would not know it that night but it was the development of a disease called Multiple Sclerosis that would give us challenges that never seemed to quit coming. It was the night I would walk with the doctor in the parking lot of his office complex, torn between the perfect evening temperatures and a great concern for my wife. This doctor was a man who had become a friend as well as our physician. I had never had anyone in the medical field who just wanted to walk and talk before, but I knew his heart was heavy. We walked and talked some, but mostly walked, while he tried to gain the courage to tell me that he could do no more. My heart dropped to the pavement as I heard him finally tell me he didn't know what to do next. He didn't know what was wrong.

We would eventually discover what was happening to Jackie. This disease had started its secret command of my beautiful wife's body years prior to a permanent disclosure of symptoms that would test our emotions, peculiarly, but very subtlety this night. It would taunt us for thirty-three years by bringing great pain and confusion. It would at times seemingly go away, but it was really hiding for just the right time to reappear. It would be a night that would test, but not break, my spiritual conviction of God being who He is. A night when everything I had been through, everything I had learned, everything from my heritage, everything I knew, was on trial against what I did not know. In every part of my thinking process, my emotions, and even physically, it seemed the dark night could not get any darker. I also knew in a few hours I must stand in the pulpit and tell everyone how good God is. While it seems to be a difficult statement to have to make at a time like that, it was the right thing to do because even when we hurt, He is still a God who loves us. Even when we seem to have no answers, He is still the One we go to with our questions.

I did not know what to tell our children; I did not know what to tell our parents; I did not know what to tell the church or anyone. I look back on that night with mixed emotions. It was a beautiful desert evening. The temperature was perfect. The sky was clear of any obstruction to the stars. The humidity was perfect. It was a perfect night for a couple to hold hands and take a walk, but it would not be what I would have the joy of doing. It would be several years before I would ask God to help me fully trust Him, but that night was another step in my journey to trusting God. In time it would eventually change my life. I felt as if I was caught in a dust devil - constantly going in circles, while not bodily, but in my mind, in my thoughts.

The dust devils we had in Ohio was just some dust that gets caught in the wind that is turning in circles. It took on a new meaning in the desert. The sand at times could be harsh and would sting. The tumble weed sometimes got caught in the swirling wind, giving it no choice but to become part of the dust devil. Wherever the wind would blow, the tumble weed was pushed to go. I felt much like that. No control, no way to fix it, no idea what to fix, and what seemed even more frustrating, this doctor whom we knew so well and who cared about us, had no answers. My mind would continue to swirl with emotional stress, seeking something that could give me a clue of what to do. "Please somebody tell me what to do. We are young. This is not supposed to happen to someone our age." I am now faced with a new dilemma and I can't fix it. I have never had to face decision-making situations like this before. What do I do? It is amazing the things we see when we look back after we have had to clumsily go forward.

After we had been through the initial shock, spending time with many doctors and still not getting answers, or at least the ones we wanted to hear, Jackie seemed to get a little better. She was able to get around on a walker, but she didn't want to break away from her comfort zone, which was mostly the house. I realized I needed to get her out to see the beauty of the desert once again. This is the place God called us to minister and we had come to love it so much. I knew she needed to once again discover the beauty of the mountains that seemed to reach into the heavens. She needed to see the desert landscape that could take creatures and creation from a hot environment and make it look so unique that it would bring a loss of words to the most eloquent speaker.

I then had a brilliant idea. I would take Jackie out to lunch. I would take her to one of our favorite places. We could not afford the expensive dining cuisines, but we had places we could afford that had good food. Jackie would resist leaving the house, but I would answer all her objections with the right answer. She would have to take her walker through crowds of people, and I said we would go at lunch time and maybe they wouldn't be as busy. It would take longer for her to get ready and then there were other excuses, but finally she realized I was not budging on this one. I had made my decision. She finally agreed and so we set about the details to make it happen. I am quite confident that by this time I had been elevated to the status of genius by making this happen. We arrived at the restaurant, and I had a big smile on my face because I knew this would be the day everything changes for the positive. I put on the hero t-shirt because I had done it again. I stepped from our car, helped my beautiful wife out of the car; then walking slowly with her across the parking lot to the restaurant, I suddenly had a revelation. This day of much needed time of togetherness across a table for lunch was also a day that my brain had a good thought but failed me at this most desperate time. Why would I say that? I'm glad you asked. We were going to a place that is often very busy because the food was very good and abundant. One of the best restaurants of its kind in any state, but one very important piece of information had escaped my memory. I am standing in the parking lot, a member of the detailed person's club, realizing I was taking my lovely wife to a *smorgasbord*, a *buffet*, all you can eat but you have to serve yourself if you want to eat place! Jackie could barely walk, how would she get her food from the food bar, and how was that going to make her feel, knowing she couldn't carry it. I stopped in the middle of the parking lot, looked at my beautiful bride and confessed that it did not enter my fragile mind that this was probably not the best, most convenient place to take her. I asked her if she wanted to go somewhere else, and of course being the gentle loving person she was, she told me it would be ok. We would stay. I continued to help her into the restaurant, bumping my dunce hat on the door header as we walked in.

God is so good. The Lord had planned ahead knowing my heart was in the right place even if I had missed a few other small details. We were practically all alone in the huge restaurant. It was lunchtime in a popular spot to eat, and we only had to share this long table of deliciously prepared food with a couple of other people. The scarcity of people in this restaurant was so unusual that I couldn't help but wonder if there was something I was missing. It had been a while since we had been there. Did I miss something in the paper about this place? I helped Jackie to a table close to the food bar where I could ask her what she would like to have. I did not have to talk loudly because our table was so close. That day of unusually empty seats, scarcity of customers, and more good food than we could describe was the day we would enjoy a lunch that would help Jackie begin to make public, this dreaded disease that was now hers for the rest of her life. That day would begin a confidence in her that she did not have to hide from the rest of the world. If someone had a problem with her apparent disability, it was in fact their problem. She did not have to shoulder someone else's inability to handle what could not be changed and would also become a witness. The time would come when Jackie would not be able to walk into a restaurant. Not only would she have to ride into the building in a wheelchair, but she would also have to be fed. Did it take some adjustment? Yes.

I want to tell you a story that revealed one of the ways God was using this disease. Once when we were traveling, we had stopped at a restaurant for dinner. As we sat there eating, a lady stopped at our table as she was leaving. She simply said to Jackie, "You are such a blessing," and then she walked on. Satan took that opportunity to try to make me feel sorry for myself by trying to get me to question why my efforts were not a blessing. His demonic suggestion was that since I was the caregiver, I was the one who fed her; I was the one who had to help her dress; I was the one that got her ready for her day; I was the one who did double duty for most all her needs, and it didn't even get me a "good job" or a smile in my direction! Maybe I could have had at least a pat on the back or something? Thank God I didn't succumb to the temptation to pity myself. I realized that the girl I loved sitting across from me would patiently wait for me to feed her and still keep a smile on her face. I would imagine this lady saw us giving thanks, my feeding Jackie, and the smile on Jackie's face which said to this stranger, that in spite of what life brings, we can still love each other as well as loving the giver of life. We have no idea what God was saying to that lady. We don't know what she was facing. Is it possible that God put us at that table, in that restaurant, at that time to speak to the heart of this person we would probably only see once in this life? Some would say that was just a coincidence. Maybe it was, but as a friend told me once, the definition of coincidence is when God chooses to be anonymous. Now in considering what the enemy was trying to do to my attitude, it is common for true caregivers to sometimes wonder if people see them. It is a fact that most people do not know to what extent a person must go to give someone assistance so they can have the best life possible. This is where the big question can be relevant. Why do we do it? Is it out of duty or love? I can only answer for myself. That answer was given on June 22, 1968, when we were married. It started from the moment I met Jackie, to the moment of our first date, to the first time I told her I loved her, to our wedding day where we both affirmed we would keep each other in sickness and in health. Do I think she would have done the same for me if I had been the one with the disease? I know she would have. The commitments we made that day were until death we part. The promises we gave in front of all those people that special day was our assurance of becoming one, and we didn't say it lightly.

Another question that is often asked is how could anyone be in love with a God who would allow something like this disease to happen? I do have an answer for that question. It is a contention that arises quite often, but for now

I will leave it at this. The way a person can love and trust God is, they are assured that in Christ a disease can only go to the end of this life, not into eternity from this life. Thanks to God who lives!

CHAPTER 10

Trust from Pain and Confrontation

We moved back from Tucson, Arizona in January of 1987 to Westerville, Ohio. Jackie was still not doing well, and we thought that it might help her to be around more of the family. As you already know, we loved it in Tucson, but Jackie's care was more important. I had no idea at that point that our moving back was just another part of God's plan to further Jackie's ministry. We moved into a house that Jackie's parents found for us to rent. It was a nice house, not as big as the one where we lived in Tucson, but we would be happy there and once again, everything fit. It also was in a cul-de-sac and we liked that. We had good neighbors, and Jackie soon got to know the lady a couple doors from us. She was very nice and was having some physical problems as well. She told Jackie several times how encouraging she was to her. Jackie, of course, would continue her life of praise for the Lord and how He had always been so good to us. Jackie was not a complainer, but instead she would be a witness.

I worked in different situations for a while trying to make ends meet. It was not long that I found myself back in the building business. It usually takes a while to build a reputation so people will trust you enough to allow you to be in their homes when they are not there while you do the work, but God was good and once again made work available. Times were difficult. We had food to eat and a dry place to eat it, but there wasn't any extra. To some we would have been considered rich, and to others we would have been called poor. During the five years we would live in this house, there would be one year when I had to tell the kids there was no money for presents for them or the family at Christmas. That was very difficult because I love giving gifts. That year I had to learn what it meant to receive without being able to give. I would have to sit on the sidelines and watch while others got that blessing this time. The church we were attending found out about our situation and took up a love offering for us to be able to have something for Christmas. We didn't know it was for us until they gave us the gift of money. We had never faced this part of life before.

It is said there are two kinds of people in this world, givers and takers. We had always tried to be givers, but when you have no choice than to be a receiver, it helps you understand how to be a better giver. Not everyone who receives is a taker. Sometimes for reasons out of their control, necessity creates a receiver. This was a new challenge for us as a family, but also it would be a blessing and a lesson we would never forget.

One time the clothes dryer quit working and since I had worked in an appliance shop while in college, I decided to fix it. I took it apart and found that the heating coil in the back was broken. I checked on the cost of replacing it and knew I could not afford to buy a new coil, so I had to fix it. I told Jackie I was not sure how long this patch job would work, but for now it was working. I want you to know I never had to replace the heating coil as long as we had the dryer. Thank the Lord once again.

Jackie was no longer able to physically work outside the home, but she was able to continue to do some cleaning. Our house was spotless because Jackie was very particular about her house. She would also be able to cook some of the time, and laundry was always on the agenda. We wanted her to be able to stay home for the kids anyway, so we tried to make that happen most of our married life. I really did believe God was in control of all things including our lives, but some days were a little more difficult than others to keep that perspective.

I very vividly remember one morning during my prayer time before I left for work when I was mostly praying, maybe a little complaining, but still I was trying to talk to God. I was telling Him how difficult things were, as if He didn't know, when suddenly I said to God, "Teach me to trust You." I stopped, looked around, and wondered where that came from. Then I realized what I had said. I thought that is a good idea so I said it again. "God, teach me to trust You." I was proud of that statement and instantly knew how God was going to teach me this wonderful, valuable, lifesaving, financially life-altering lesson!

I am like anyone else who likes to be right and that morning was no exception. I love it when I take something to God and I already know how He is going to do it. I knew instantly when I asked Him to teach me to trust Him that God was either going to make my construction business grow to the point where all I had to do was to drive around in a four- wheel drive truck with a new cell phone making sure all the jobs were being done right, or someone would pull up in front of my house with a huge check from some contest. I knew that God had already started working on the answer just this way and all that was left for me to do was to wait a couple of days.

There is a song that says,

"The answer's on its way!"

I was sure everything was in motion now. Which one would it be? Would it be the big check or more business than I could imagine?

I also don't like being wrong. My business did not grow as I thought it would, although I was busy and able to pay our bills. I did not get a big check and no mobile phone. I did, however, in the midst of being able to meet my obligations encounter challenges that seemed to run together. They would test me in ways I never want to endure again, and taught me a lesson I could not have learned any other way. It was about eight months later. I was back at the same place, whining, and crying about how tough we had it when God said something that changed my life. He said to me, "You asked Me to teach you to trust Me, didn't you?" I very quickly questioned what that had to do with anything I was talking to Him about right then. My business didn't grow. I could not get a cell phone. Furthermore, I was not able to purchase my four-wheel drive truck. No one pulled up in front of my house with a million dollar check. I asked God, "What is this about? Why are you asking this question?" I thought we had already settled what would, and should have happened to get us out of this barnyard life. What I was about to find out was that God not only sees the big picture, He is the big picture. He was about to show me a valuable lesson. The song we would hear sung later, written by Lawrence Chewning in 1992 about challenges he and his wife went through, titled "The Anchor Holds" would become a part of our testimony. I would try to sing all the way through it but the part that states, "it was in the night through the storms of my life oh that's when God proved His love to me, and the anchor holds" was hard to get through without tears or great emotion.

The Father was in the process of letting me see a glimpse of a life that can be painful to live, but oh, so important. Something that would not have man's hands on it anywhere. I would never be the same. I was about to learn one of the most valuable lessons I could learn. It would mean more to me and to those that I would encounter than I had ever conceived possible.

The morning I was complaining to God about how difficult our life was, He said to me," You asked Me to teach you to trust Me, didn't you"? At this point He was trying to bring my attention back to what was important for me to see. He wanted me to learn from the difficult days of life. Then He said, "You have had to, haven't you?" While I thought about what that meant for me and my family, I realized I was still building a relationship with the Lord of my heritage. It was about my surrendering, my learning, and the act of obedience. I was trusting God, but didn't really know what I was doing. I realized at that moment what it really meant to trust Him. God had allowed me to be in a place where, while unconsciously I had trusted God for all my needs, I would now seek a relationship with Him that would allow Him to care for everything in my life. I had been a Christian for many years already. How did it escape me that I wasn't thinking that He gives us each breath, each heartbeat, and instead we still think we have to carry everything on our shoulders. To trust Him means that I must give my need to Him and take my hands off. He was the one that had taken care of us through every valley and across every mountain. I was no better or worse materially than when I asked Him to teach me to trust Him. We still had food to eat and a place to live. My efforts had not developed anything better. There was only one Person who had provided for our needs in the last eight months. Father God may use others to accomplish what He wants, but it is all Him. He meets our needs.

The inspired song, "Trust and Obey", fits very well here. As told by the late Cliff Barrows about this song,

"Trust and Obey"

The music for this song was composed by D. B. Towner, the first director of music at Moody Bible Institute in Chicago.

The inspiration for the hymn's writing came in 1886 during an occasion when Towner was leading singing for D. L. Moody in Brockton, Massachusetts. In a testimony service, he heard a young man say, "I am not quite sure – but I am going to trust, and I am going to obey."

Towner jotted down the words and sent them to his friend J. H. Sammis, a Presbyterian minister, who developed the idea into a full hymn.

The refrain came first – it is a capsule version of the entire song – and the verse later.

D. L. Moody said in one occasion: "The blood (of Christ) alone makes us safe. The Word (of God) alone makes us sure. Obedience (to God) makes us happy."

CHAPTER 11
You Want Me to do What?

Did you ever just want to ask God a question but you were afraid to? Maybe the question sounded something like this, "You want me to do what?" Sometimes the appropriate question is," Why?" or, "Are you sure?" The question may be something totally different, but the important point is we can ask God anything we want. We may have no problem asking these questions to our spouse, our parents, our friend or any other person but if it is Father God, we may have some fear in asking. I find it interesting we are afraid to talk to the Father about what we are thinking or feeling, as if He doesn't already know what we have on our heart and mind. We say in one breath He knows all, and then we think we can keep our thoughts from Him. I have found I can talk to the Father about anything. He knew about it before I did so there was no reason not to talk with Him about something in my life. I may have a question or something may be troubling me, but He is already aware of it! There is no one who cares more about my hearing, understanding, and following truth than the Father. There is no one who loves me more than the Father. He wants me to be what He wants me to be. He wants me to trust Him, to walk and talk with Him, because He knows what is best for me, and you. He gave His Son for us, so why do we think we can't talk to Him about questions we have? What about our challenges, our pain or something we don't like about life? If we trust our Father, we can, and should talk to Him. I have been asked what it means to say we talk to God. The NKJV Bible says in Genesis 1:26, Let Us make man in Our image, according to Our likeness. We are made in God's image. We also find in Genesis 1:28 and 29, where God's word says, Then God blessed them, and God said to them. In verse 29 again His words are recorded to say, And God said. If He says it, and He will, there must be a way for us to hear Him say it. If we are created in His image, then it must be because He wants to communicate with us. If we believe He is God, then it is to our advantage to believe He chooses to be a part of our lives, twenty-four hours a day, and seven days a week.

Newborns are amazing. When my granddaughter was born she wasn't much bigger than a football and as I sat there holding her, I was also the one crying nearly nonstop. I was sitting there holding a miracle. I am not just talking about the miracle of reproduction; I am talking about the fact that her daddy, our son was also a miracle baby.

Without answered pray, Todd and his sister Kelly would not be alive. I sat and held her while crying because she is our fourth grandchild, but she was the first to be born alive. I sat there crying not just because of the past, but also because of how beautiful she was. I sat there holding her with excitement of what her future could be. I was sitting, holding my granddaughter while I softly talked to her even though at the moment she had no way of communicating with me and yet she seemed to be very content in my hands, or cuddled in my arms. She will have words to communicate as she develops and when she is capable of understanding what I am saying to her, she will respond. The time will come when she and I will have a dialog. She already feels safe as I talk to her because I choose my words and my tone correctly, lovingly, so she is not afraid. Now that she is older, I have had the joy of teaching her new words, and seeing her climb out of her crib when we thought it was too early. We were never ready for that one. I have enjoyed watching her eyes and her actions at her first Christmas when she was more interested in the boxes the presents came in and the little $5 snow shovel than all the money spent for everything else. I got excited about a phone call when she was trying to tell me about her using her little pot for the first time. I must say it was in a language not yet discovered. I remember when she began to learn to talk, and we would laugh together about silly things that have nothing to do with anything. I remember when she started to school and I was reminded of when her daddy and aunt started to school. I got to watch as she would grab her little brother's hand to help him. I was blessed to be at some of her birthday parties with her friends and watch her involved in everything possible. I loved asking her if she was still Papa's girl and she would answer, "Yes" while she got real tight under my protective arm. If I have been able to enjoy all that and more, how much does our Heavenly Father enjoy being with us, when we will include Him? If I am able to communicate with my children and grandchildren and love them, how much more should we understand that the Creator wants that special time with us? Our past is important, so what about the development of our future? I am concerned about who my grandchildren choose as help mates. I'm interested in their schooling and where they go to college. I pray for the choices they make to be God's will. If I care that much, how much more is the author of love interested in our life choices? If we accept that He loves us that much, doesn't it make sense He would want to communicate with us? We have His Word that helps us understand His character, His laws, and His promises, just to name a few, so doesn't it make sense He will communicate with us? The real question is, will we listen and would we recognize His voice?

KJV John 10:1 Verily, verily, I say unto you, He that entereth not by the door into the sheepfold, but climbeth up some other way, the same is a thief and a robber.

John 10:2 But he that entereth in by the door is the shepherd of the sheep.

John 10:3 To him the porter openeth; and the sheep hear his voice: and he calleth his own sheep by name, and leadeth them out.

John 10:4 And when he putteth forth his own sheep, he goeth before them, and the sheep follow him: for they know his voice.

John 10:5 And a stranger will they not follow, but will flee from him: for they know not the voice of strangers.

I remember the first time I was on a roller-coaster. I also remember the second time I rode a roller-coaster, and there were a lot of years separating the two times. My first time was an impulsive decision when I was a senior in high school, and my second was when my children wanted me to ride with them. My first time was when a good friend and I were trying to meet two girls. When we got off the ride, after sitting in the front car, second seat, I told my buddy," Let's get out of here. No girl is worth another ride on that." I quickly was considering my priorities. My second ride was because I loved my son and daughter, and I wanted to experience something with them. I even stood in a long line waiting to get on it. Once again I had considered my priorities. I tell you this story as an illustration of learning to listen to our Father. I want to know His will because of my love for Him. I want to be what He wants me to be so I can do what He wants me to do. When He asks me to do something, I want to be able to hear and recognize His voice. I want to make that decision to obey Him because I already trust Him. That decision is a priority to me. He will not ask me to be or do something that will hurt me or my family. When God led Jackie and me to take our son, Todd, and go back to Circleville Bible College, we knew the Father had a reason in leading us to do that. This was Todd's senior year in high school. This would give him some obvious challenges by changing schools. An interesting comment from Todd helped us to see how God was working in our lives for yet another change. We were talking to him about what we were considering and then with no consideration or connection to our subject he said, "I feel like I have fallen back in love with Jesus." Jackie and I looked at each other and agreed we were following God's plan.

I love to learn, but I didn't love the classroom. Yet here God was leading me to finish my degree, but this was not the only reason I was saying, "You want me to do what?" There would be ministry God would lead us to do during the time at the college which would bring more challenges. It wasn't always easy.

One of the blessings we would have was for the next five years Jackie and I would have the privilege of being the boys' dorm parents. During that time with the boys, God used Jackie to touch more lives as "Mom" in our dorm and to some girls that came to visit. It was a good five years, but I couldn't help but wonder how long we would be there. We had come to joyfully accept wherever God led us, to be content and to buckle up for the ride.

After we had been there five years, God began to shuffle our lives again. We took a position with Brown Road Community Church. I remember talking to the pastor many times about the future. The pastor and I both knew Jackie and I were supposed to be a part of the church at that point, but we also knew it wasn't long term. There were times when I would ask him if he had a revelation for me, but he didn't. It was a help to know he knew our time there was temporary, but a test to my patience, too.

While at Brown Road Community Church as the associate pastor, I supplemented my income by working in construction again. God opened the door for me to return to Circleville Bible College to do some building there. I had no idea that this construction occupation would lead to our next step.

While we were at Circleville Bible College, God began to orchestrate our calling to the American Indian field. This opportunity would facilitate Jackie's witness reaching more people than ever before. One of the projects I had to build was a townhouse for married students to live in. It would also be a project to supply World Gospel Mission a facility for student activities, and an apartment for their director of student development. My contact for this project would stop by from time to time, and one day I asked him if he knew what they were doing for maintenance people on the American Indian field. I told him I was just curious. I did not have any reason to feel the Lord would ever be interested in having us go there, so this was not a divinely inspired question. I was just curious and at that point it was just inquisitiveness. Sometimes God activates our interest before He makes it a calling for our life. He told me he did not know what their needs were and suggested that I call Frank Brown. Well, I had many years of experience in construction work and thought it would be interesting to get to do something on the American Indian field. I was still not going to say this was a divinely inspired thought or question. We had been at the school in Arizona several times and so it was a normal inquiry, besides how would we ever be able to do something like that? I was fifty years old and Jackie had been diagnosed with Multiple Sclerosis.

Multiple Sclerosis, hereafter I will refer to it as MS, causes lesions of the myelin sheath that covers the nerves. I must confess I am not a doctor, but I did a lot of research on this debilitating disease Jackie now had. For those interested, I will try to give a little insight into what I have learned. I will illustrate a lesion as being comparable to a crack in the insulation of an electric wire. When an electric wire is in use, it is carrying energy through the insulated copper wire. If there is a crack present in the insulation, it can short out and carry the energy most likely in a different path. In the world of electric, an opening in the insulation can do damage to whatever is around it. In the body, when the myelin sheath has a crack in it, better known as a lesion, the signal the nerve is trying to carry from the brain is to a point the brain has determined. That signal can be diverted to another part of the body. This can cause one of the symptoms that Jackie had called, intentional tremors. The lesions in the brain can cause other symptoms depending on the severity of the lesions. There are people who may never show a symptom of MS but they still have the disease. Jackie happened to have multiple symptoms. Her eyesight was affected, and eventually even the control of her eye was affected. She would eventually have pain. Her speech was affected. She had tremors and had loss of strength and co-ordination. Her short term memory was affected. Her ability to clearly think things through was affected. The control of her body was affected and she could not feed herself. That is enough to make a person bitter, to question God's existence, and if He does exist, does He really care? Jackie did not suggest she had that question or feel that way one time in her life. In the beginning of this disease we would sit and just hold each other, often crying, sometimes late into the night. Jackie would continue to praise God for His love and thank Him for the blessings He bestowed on us. She continued moving forward to serve Him in as many capacities as possible until her body was just not able to keep pushing. She understood and was very much aware that God could heal her here, or one day she would be fully healed in His presence.

Jackie once said, while with a group of people, that one day when she got to heaven she would not walk into heaven, she would run. A friend of ours, who was blind and had been since birth, told her he was going to watch her run in heaven. Some of you might be questioning if we really felt that way. When Jackie was first experiencing the physical difficulties that we later learned was MS, we were faced with the question, how would we deal with this change in our lives? We had two children and at that time they were twelve and nine; Jackie and I were still young but we had no idea how this disease was going to affect our lives. The reality is that when a spouse, parent, or child gets a disease, it can seem like the rest of the family members also have it. One person may have the disease, but it influences the family and how they handle the choices they must make, as well. It is not uncommon for people not to know how to handle what they see. Fear of doing something wrong can distance people when at that most critical time the family that is hurting needs people to express their love to them. Sometimes the person with the disease does not know how to communicate their feelings, and that may lead them to become more introverted. Having a close friend to be more proactive in their life can be lifesaving. Jackie was blessed to have such a friend. Instead of taking the path that some well-meaning people took when they would say "let me know if you need something," or "if I can do something for you, let me know," this friend of ours would come to our home in Tucson after she got off work even before she went home to care for her own family. She wanted to know what she was to do. She didn't ask if there was something to do, but in fact, what do you need me to do today?

While I do not want to leave the impression that those who did not ask the question or come by with that direct of intent did not care, but we were in a crisis mode. We were trying to comprehend how to handle life. It might have been nice to have a flood of people at our door insisting they were there to do something for us, but I'm not sure we could have managed too many at a time. This disease was so foreign to us; we didn't know what to do. MS does not come with an instruction manual, any more than raising children does. We had to learn by trial and a lot of error. We did not have anyone living close to us that was facing the same symptoms as Jackie, so there was no one to talk to that could encourage us from their experience. Some would say, "I know how you feel" when Jackie would say how tired she was. That was not very comforting, and sometimes left us shaking our heads. No matter what experiences a person has had, we do not know how someone else feels! We may want to think we know how someone who is dealing with a difficult situation feels, but since God made each of us unique, we handle life's challenges differently. We knew people were trying to be helpful and kind but there is a real lesson here that should be addressed.

When you see someone that is hurting, see what you can do to ease their stress, and pain. Pain is not always physical, but pain hurts no matter how it gets there. Life is not just about the person wearing our skin. If it is someone in the position we were in, maybe a home cooked meal would be helpful. Maybe arrange for someone to come and stay with the family for an evening. Make it possible for the caretaker to get out for a little while to take in a ball game, go shopping, or just do something out of the daily routine. Maybe the caretaker would like to take the kids to the park or the zoo, but they need someone to stay with their spouse so they can do that. Maybe a few people could cooperate together to help clean the house or mow the grass. The caretaker could very well be a person that doesn't want to take advantage of anyone, so how you offer your help will determine whether they will allow you to do it. I know from experience. Most people in this position are already dealing with a lot of emotion, questions, and stress. Be sensitive to people and their feelings. The last recognition they need is to stand out like a bald man at an Elvis impersonator convention. Someone reading this may be thinking they are too quiet and backward to approach the caregiver. I would suggest getting another person on your team who is not afraid to be assertive. Make it about the person in need and not about you. The opportunity to minister when people are hurting can be a lasting experience for everyone involved.

At this point, someone may ask the question that Satan tried to get us to ask, "Where is God?" In Psalm 13 David asks the question in the first two verses, "how long" four times. There were times when that question seemed to be appropriate and yet God never failed us. Not once did He forsake us and never was He displeased because we asked questions from lack of understanding. I will confess that when God taught me what it meant to really trust Him, I realized I didn't need to understand as much about life situations. It is especially true when a person can't do anything about their condition. I also discovered I didn't ask the question "why?" as much. God was and is always there. Yes, a disease affects the whole family in some way but how we handle our part of it is an individual decision.

Well, back to what God wanted us to do next. Go to a mission field? This is where the title of a book that Stan Toler wrote *I Love God's Sense of Humor; I Just Wish He'd Let Me in on the Joke* is appropriate. How could we handle the demands of a mission field? Who would want a couple in our situation, and surely God could not be a part of something like this. I was asking what they were doing for maintenance people just because I was curious. Nothing divinely inspired going on here. Just curiosity, but my curiosity was not diminishing so I thought maybe I would try to get in touch with Frank Brown one of these days just to see what he had to say.

A couple of days later one of the guys and I walked into the back door of the kitchen at the college looking for cookies and were greeted by our cook. She was a good friend and usually busy, but many times she would have cookies on racks to cool. We would volunteer to sample the cookies because we understood quality control is the success of any operation, and we wanted to do our part to help out. As we were getting our cookies, we noticed she was all smiles. I could not help but wonder what was making her day so special, and it was not long until she told me. I found out that the next day she had a meeting scheduled with the same person I needed to contact, Frank Brown. Of course, I was shocked and then I asked her to make sure that I got a chance to see him. Some people would call that a coincidence. Again the definition of coincidence is when God chooses to be anonymous. I didn't know she was considering missions and she didn't know I needed to talk to Frank, but God knew what pieces had to be put together. He knew it was necessary for me to talk to Frank because I was about to make a major purchase.

I remember the day Frank came as if it just happened. Just a few weeks before, I decided to buy the backhoe that I had been leasing to do the work I was doing for the college. It appeared that construction was the direction things were going for me, again, so I figured when I finished with the work I was doing for the college I could use some more equipment. I did have one concern. A few months earlier I had tried to buy a dump truck and the bank turned me down. I had no idea why my application was turned down and they never gave me a good reason. Everything was in order and there should have been no problem but they said, "No." I told the backhoe salesman about the truck and the possibility my application would not be accepted. I had no idea why I could not get the money for the dump truck and this backhoe was going to cost a lot more money than the truck would have. I had more than one project we were working on at that time, so when Frank stopped to see me there were many people around the job site that day, but Frank was very patient. I was arranging the crew to keep the work going so we could go to our house where Jackie, Frank and I could talk. Just as we were about to leave the job site, the backhoe sales representative arrived, a day early. He had told me it would take a few days to get the application processed, but there he was. I went over and sat in his car to hear him tell me that the paper work had gone through without a hitch, in fact, it was quicker than he thought it would be. All I had to do was sign the papers. Now the big question here is, "What do I do?" I said to him," I am sorry you drove out today because I cannot sign the papers today."

"In fact," I told him, "what I do in the future may depend on what that man tells us," and I pointed to Frank. The salesman was a Christian and he said, "No problem, I will call you tomorrow." Frank went down to the house to talk with Jackie and me about the mission field.

I must say I was a little surprised the way our conversation progressed. Remember, we were not what I would call the typical candidates to go to the mission field. I was fifty years old and Jackie had a disease that was unpredictable to deal with at times, but here is where the story gets more interesting. There was no doubt in our minds that God wanted us to be a part of something, and we were about to learn a small part of what it was.

I want to insert here God had helped us to "be" instead of just doing. To do does not require a person to be spiritual, but to be ready, be willing, and to be sold out to Christ requires surrender of self. To be sold out to Christ is to be available for whatever He wants from us. God had helped us come to a place where we were willing to say "yes" and then trust God for what was unknown. When God told me He was going to use Jackie's disease for ministry, I had no idea what that meant.

We were not the only ones who wondered what God was up to. I know of at least one person who thought it was unrealistic for us to pursue such a task. I can only wonder how many other people were thinking the same thing.

The problem can be that we look through eyes that are restricted. We are not able to see the big picture as God does. If we are not able to trust God fully, then we have difficulty trusting Him with what insight He gives us. When God taught me what it meant to trust Him, He would also help me to see His majestic character, His trustworthiness, His love, His ability to be complete. I had experienced what He could do many times before this venture. Now we were about to experience a bigger step in life and it would not just be for us. God works through those who will let Him so others can see His greatness, and sometimes it will also be for the benefit of the believer.

We submitted an application to become missionaries, and we were denied our request for career missionary status. We were, however, encouraged by Dr. Tom Hermiz, who was at that time the President of World Gospel Mission, to seek volunteer status. We decided to take the volunteer status and worked with Frank Brown once again on the details. We would still have to raise funds to go as volunteers on the mission field. We didn't have enough money to live on without working so we proceeded to raise our funds, and within ten months we had our support raised. To God is the glory! Was it easy? No. However, we determined that we would try to minister everywhere we went and not just to raise money.

We traveled to many different churches preaching the gospel message, trying to raise our support, and doing our best to show people that God can use anyone who is willing to say "yes". When God calls those who by society's measuring stick are the qualified, where is the unusual in that? When God qualifies the called, helps those who think they have nothing to offer to do His bidding for the kingdom, then God is glorified. When people who are not expected to accomplish much excel in the Lord, and give Him glory for doing it, it baffles the status quo crowd. When a person is willing to trust God to do through them what would seem impossible, God is able to be a blessing to the willing servant, as well as perplexing to the skeptic. I know I am not the best preacher we have, and we knew we would never win a Dove award for our music, but that was not what we were there to do. God opened the opportunity for Jackie and me to try to touch people's lives, and that is why we were there. So while we were trying to raise our support to go to the mission field we would tell the people the best we could what we would be doing there. We would tell them a little bit about the American Indian field, sing and then present the gospel. I have heard some say no one gets saved at a missionary service. I beg to differ. God blessed us with people at the altar being saved, surrendering to God's Holy Spirit, becoming more committed to the work of Christ, while committing more deeply to missions. This happened in many of our services. How dare we limit what God can do?

I remember one man who told me he had been guilty of saying, "Lord, why are they going to the mission field? What is Jackie going to be able to do in the condition she is in?" I asked him what God's answer was. He told me that God's answer to him was that it was none of his business what we were going to do, but he was going to help support the Amlins. He told me he lost sleep until he agreed to support us. I want to say here that this was a good man who just verbalized what I feel more people were thinking. The focus sometimes can be what you can do rather than what God can do through you.

In August of 1999, the last project I was responsible for at the campus was just about finished. It was because of the many hours of volunteers, a small crew, a lot of hard work, and patience.

It was time for us to move west again. The move this time would be to the American Indian field in Arizona. We had raised all our support; everything was complete and ready for us to head out. As you know, we lived in Arizona once before and we loved it there. However, this was a completely different move. We would be going to Peoria where the Southwest Indian Ministries Center was located which is a part of the Phoenix area, called the Valley of the Sun. We would be entering an exciting ministry but one in which we had no experience. We would be working with different tribes of the Native American people.

Jackie and I instantly fell in love with the Native American people. We also loved where we lived, we loved the work we were doing, and so we decided we would never leave. Our goal was to walk through the doors God opened for us as volunteer missionaries on the American Indian field until those doors closed and locked. It was not too many months until World Gospel Mission asked us to consider the position of fulltime career missionaries. We knew that accepting career status would mean that we would have to raise more support. Therefore, we started to put a plan together to move back to Ohio for a short time to raise the extra support.

About January of that year, Jackie started having some other physical problems not related to the Multiple Sclerosis, and also I got a call from my mother from Florida that indicated there was something happening with my father. She did not ask me to come to Florida, where they wintered, but I could tell she needed me. I said to our acting field director that I needed to fly to Florida to check on my dad.

In those days, Jackie could stay by herself, but some of the missionaries would stop in to check on her and help her. They may need to take her where she needed to go off campus, but she had her golf cart to get around on campus. Most of Jackie's prayer ministry, she could do at home.

I made provisions to fly to Florida to help my parents knowing Jackie would be fine. I got my father to a doctor who quickly ordered a CAT scan, which showed to us that he had a tumor in the brain. It was a difficult time for all of us. I should admit here, I was starting to wonder how many difficult things can actually go together at one time. The next one I had to face was to tell my mother and father what was found on the CAT scan because the doctor didn't want to do it. It was one of the hardest things that I have ever had to do. The doctor ordered an MRI for the next day and it confirmed he had a brain tumor. The doctors suggested that I drive Mom and Dad back to Ohio and of course, since we didn't know the progression of the tumor for sure, we flew Jackie to Ohio from Arizona.

After the doctor's visits, testing, and discovering that Dad only had a short time to live, Jackie and I decided we needed to go back to Arizona to get our truck and clothes. We also had to see her doctor about the new physical complications she was facing.

Our supervisor at World Gospel Mission had already said that we could leave early on furlough so we could be with Dad since he had such a short time to live.

We flew back to Arizona on Monday, went to Jackie's doctor's appointment only to be informed by Jackie's doctor that she would have to have major surgery. Again I refer to a book by Stan Toler, called *God Has Never Failed Me, But He's Sure Scared Me To Death A Few Times*. I think of this book often and especially the title. Can you guess that this is one of those times? We discussed with the doctor the possibility of Jackie having the surgery in Ohio and shared with him about my father's situation. He said he would agree to the surgery in Ohio if they would do the procedure a certain way. My sister, who has been such a blessing over the years, had a very responsible position in teaching nursing at the Springfield Community Hospital. Her thirty plus years of having the responsibility of caring for patients, teaching, and her reputation in the community among many doctors and specialists made it helpful in her making arrangements for an excellent surgeon in caring for Jackie's needs. This surgeon even consulted with the doctor in Arizona and then made all the arrangements for the procedure. We had two weeks to store all of our furniture and belongings on the American Indian field, prepare for others to handle our responsibilities on the field and leave for Ohio.

On Saturday, we drove to Pearce, Arizona where we were to have two services the next morning at Wynn Chapel and then leave for Ohio. On Monday morning we headed east, quite exhausted and yet knew that we had to get there as quickly as we could because of my father's illness and Jackie's upcoming surgery. One day we could only travel 300 miles because we were so tired. That morning we were slow getting out of the motel. I was having a hard time since my "get up and go" had not yet arrived from the day before. It is amazing how God works. While it is true we were having a difficult time getting on our way that morning, God used that time to open up the opportunity for us to speak with a couple who were facing some difficulties in their lives and they were slow getting away as well. I do not remember what our conversation with them was about that day, but I do remember as we traveled that Jackie and I had a discussion about how our time with them was no accident. I only hope that whatever we shared with them is still helping. I guess we may find out in heaven. This was another example of the importance of watching and praying for opportunities to try to make a difference.

I have always enjoyed the trip across our great land. I normally relax when I am driving but of course this particular trip was a little more stressful. We arrived in Ohio on April 6th and on April 12th Jackie had major surgery. Everything went well with her surgery, and we thank the Lord for all that He did to provide the right people in the right places to do such a great job. On April 22nd, we had our first service to begin raising the additional support we needed. Jackie did not have to be in a wheelchair all the time at that point, but we used one to make it easier for her to get around. What a great service we had that morning! God allowed us the opportunity to sing, share His blessings with the church and be a part of a time where His Holy Spirit moved upon the people. That service was such a great start to reach our needed goal, and I also took home a banana split cake. Oh yeah!

For the next few weeks, my agenda was to care for Jackie as she recuperated, and to help care for Dad. A few years earlier, I had helped Dad remodel part of their basement, so that is where we would live when we were in the area until we finished raising support and were able to drive back home to Arizona. It was amazing how Jackie recuperated. We thought she would have to stay upstairs for a while but it was not long until she was climbing the basement stairs, by herself, hanging on only to the railing. She was tough. It was a blessing to be able to care for Jackie and help my Dad in the same house. We knew that unless God healed Dad that we would not have him here with us for very long. The people who would come to spend time with him would be treated to his thanks and assurance that he was going home.

I remember the day that I came upstairs and Mom told me that Dad said he was going home. I went into the living room to talk to him and there he sat with his Bible, a lined, yellow, paper tablet and his box. The box was something he and a friend had made to hold some of the things he needed for his diabetes needs. His tablet was where Mom recorded everything pertaining to his care, and his Bible was what he lived by. I was anxious to hear if he was confused about where he was, or was it possible he had a glimpse of where he was going. I walked into the living room where he was sitting in his chair. "I understand you told Mom you are going home," I said to Dad. He answered, "Yes." I asked him if he meant here or heaven. He replied, "Heaven." I asked how he knew this and did Jesus tell him. He said, "Yes." I questioned him further by asking, "Will it be soon?" he said, "Yes." Just a brief time following our conversation was Dad's day to see Jesus. Those were days of mixed emotions knowing that he was home, and he would never have to deal with diabetes, tumors and pain medication in this world again, and yet how much we would miss him. I thank the Lord for my earthly father and the heritage God had given me. I am very thankful that all my life I had people, and especially men, around me that were an example of what a Godly person should be. Having them there was not only a blessing, but an example of what I should be for my children, for my grandchildren. Like it or not, we are someone's living example.

A few weeks later we would be in Indiana at World Gospel Mission preparing for the next step as we continue our life of missions. We were also starting to fill our schedule with services to continue raising the additional support to get back to the American Indian field. We would be very busy for the next year and from the time we left Arizona until we finished raising our support, we would travel

37,000 miles. From the middle of August, 2001 until May of 2002, not including January and half of December, Jackie and I would be in ninety different churches, attend several church camps, and with all that traveling and activity, Jackie would only miss two services. We were blessed to share with hundreds of people during that time in speaking, singing, and good old conversation. Our hope was to make a difference in lives wherever possible.

There were times when we would spend several days, and in some cases, a week in a motel, but I do not ever remember hearing Jackie complain or say this was not something she wanted to do. I remember several times Jackie would say she was tired, but I do not remember one time that she ever wanted to stop and go home. We even had our Christmas in a Chillicothe motel with our kids. I wasn't sure how festive it would be and as the Lord would have it, we had a very nice Christmas. The kids brought in food for the special meal, and we even decorated for the birthday celebration. The place where we stayed let us have a suite so we had two rooms to use, and we even had a small tree for the Christ child's birthday. It was a special time with a unique blessing for us.

January of 2002 would find us on the road for about a week, visiting a supporter and traveling to Colorado Springs for a mission's conference and training. We would stay at the conference center and attend sessions for three weeks, and Jackie did not miss one session. I did not realize it at the time but as I look back on it, I know God used that schedule, the miles, and the many services, to allow the opportunity for Jackie to inspire more people. Otherwise, we would never have traveled to Colorado Springs; we would never have met and interacted with missionary couples from other organizations and several states. After the conference, the couples that we had come to love and appreciate would be ministering all over the world. We would not have been a part of this if we had not been in missions. We would not have been in missions if we had not left the pastorate in Tucson. I had wondered several times why we needed to leave a place that we enjoyed. The reason is clear to me now. It was necessary to get Jackie in front of people who needed to see her love for Christ even in the condition of her body. I have also wondered how many people her life had touched that we have never even talked to. What did people think when we were in a restaurant and Jackie of course had to be fed? What did people think when in addition to that, they see this beautiful girl bow her head in prayer before her meal and still keep a smile on her face? A glimpse of the answer to that question was given to us a couple of times. I would like to remind you of the story of the lady that stopped at our table and told Jackie how much of a blessing she was, and then walked on. Naturally Jackie and I wondered what just happened. Another time we were in Oklahoma City eating at a Cracker Barrel and when we were finished, our server thanked us for coming to their Cracker Barrel. Jackie and I looked at each other not really understanding the direction of his conversation.

He continued to tell us that our meal was already paid for. I asked, "Who paid for it?" I was told that a man behind us had paid for our meal and did not want us to know about it. I sure wish I had ordered steak that night!

I believe people are looking for someone to show them that what is said about God can really be lived. I wonder if people watch to see how a person acts and reacts to situations in life that by all standards of human nature would give permission to complain and to have a bad attitude. Then God sends someone along who defies what the world accepts as normal and some are perplexed while some are blessed.

I remember for a couple years that God gave us the opportunity to travel from church to church to share a message of how we can trust God in difficult times. I did not realize the great need for that message. I guess I just thought everyone knew God cares about all aspects of our lives, and if we believe He is who we say He is; there isn't anything He can't do to help us.

I did not realize until recently that God used times like this to reach people that we would not reach any other way. I also did not realize the impact that Jackie's faithfulness would have on the couples that attended the conference in Colorado Springs.

Many of them would make comments such as, "Whenever we think about quitting we think about how Jackie kept going." Her influence at that conference would be taken around the world. Here was another situation where God would use a very humble servant whose greatest desire was to serve Him. She was not going to let a debilitating disease stop her. She would still push on even when the energy sometimes did not seem to be there, because her love for Him and the work that He had called us to do was more important than her own comfort.

We finished raising the support we needed in less than a year. We headed back to our house on the American Indian Field located in Peoria, Arizona at the American Indian Center. I don't think Jackie ever fully recovered physically from the 37,000 miles we traveled.

In January of 2003, I could tell that there was something else happening with Jackie physically. It appeared that some of her short-term memory was being affected as well as some ability to process thoughts. I began to seek what God wanted us to do with much prayer and concern because we did not want to leave the American Indian field. As I sought counsel from many different people, I would get the same response. Every one of them said I should take her home so she could be around our children. We loved our children and family but we did not like the thought of having to leave the mission field. It was a difficult time. A time of more mixed emotions, but we began to prepare for another 2,000-mile trip that would not hold the same excitement that we had experienced before. We were going back to our beginnings, to our family whom we dearly loved, but we were leaving what had become home to us. We were leaving people we will never forget, people who had impacted our lives.

By June of 2003 we were back in Ohio, back to Mom's house, but living there would even be more difficult because Jackie would start to experience a pain that was excruciating for her. It was one more new challenge where we didn't know what to do. One definite need was to find some help; we needed to find a doctor. The fall and spring seemed to be the worst time for her pain. We finally found a doctor that helped us understand this new situation. The trigeminal nerve was causing the problem. We had tried to help Jackie with the pain by using painkillers and cold packs, but it had been a very stressful and painful two months for her. When we met with this new doctor, he told us there was a procedure that could help with the pain. The procedure sounded delicate and tedious, but he and his staff were so helpful and comforting that we proceeded. They explained it to me this way. They would take a needle up through her jaw to the spot where the pain was, and place heat around it to insulate around the nerve. It did help but she would need the procedure done several times. During this time we were also faced with a very difficult transition. In leaving the mission field we had to have an income. I knew that I had to get a job, and yet with Jackie in such a difficult situation, and no place to live, there were just a lot of unanswered questions. We looked at many options and while days seemed to be very heavy at times, Jesus continued to remind me that He was always there. I felt at times like I was in a bad fog. I found it difficult to see where I was going. I felt like I had to deal with many situations over which I had no control. Not only that, I was finding it more difficult to discern the leading of the Holy Spirit. I will say God was faithful to keep impressing upon my mind that He had not left us, and Psalm 13 became more real than ever before. How to trust God in difficult times became more of a reality and still is today.

I refer to Psalm 13 again. It is such a great Psalm. The first two verses tell of David's complaint. I like the fact that David knew he could talk to God and tell Him how he felt. I don't think David ever took "How to pray 101." I really don't think he cared how other people perceived his conversation. He knew he was addressing the Creator who loved him, and he knew he could talk to Him from his heart because God understands the language of the heart. David was experiencing a difficult time in his life. He knew God knew about it, because God knows about everything. So why wouldn't he talk to God about it?

The second two verses are his prayer. David was not just interested in complaining to God. He also wanted God's help. He did not like what he had to go through and he wanted God to take care of it.

The fifth and sixth verses are what I like to call the "hallelujah verses". David complained to God that he had to go through this difficulty and was asking God why in the first two verses. He then prays that God will hear and answer his prayer in verses 3 and 4, but then he rings the bell in verse 5, when he tells God he trusts in Him. The answer has not yet come and David is saying, "I still trust in You." Why would he say he trusts in someone he has not seen, who doesn't seem to be listening, or at least is not doing anything about his problem at the moment? David makes this declaration in verse 6 when he tells us how God has dealt bountifully with him before. He is solidifying his confidence in Father God. God listens to the heart, so He knows everything David is thinking and feeling. David is saying to God what God already knows. I trust You! I do not know what the answer is or will be, but You do. I trust You!

I thought I knew what it meant to trust God prior to 1989, but it was not until I went through my, "How to trust God lesson," that it was real to me. I sure don't want to have to take a refresher course to learn that lesson again. I am glad that God taught me what it meant to trust Him because once again the only thing I had in my life to hang onto was that God never fails, He is never late, and He is always on time. It was once again a time when there were more questions than answers. Still there was an assurance that God was going to answer the questions at the right time. Jackie somehow had already learned that lesson. The only time I remember her asking a question that would be close to the subject of "why," is when she wondered why God wouldn't take her on home. When Jackie talked about going home, it was different from what I have heard anyone talking about going to heaven. I'm not sure if I ever heard her use the word "heaven." She always wanted to go "home." It is like "she has been there, knows what is there, and can't wait to get back," to quote a dear friend.

I went back to work for myself. Mom would remarry and move to Maryland. Since we were living in Mom's house, we really needed to find a house of our own so Mom could sell hers. This is not the only issues we had to deal with because Jackie's condition would continue to deteriorate. She was now at the point where I knew I had to have someone with her more regularly. We spent many days driving and looking at houses mostly in the Urbana area where we could be closer to my home church.

The Urbana Church of Christ in Christian Union had become such a blessing to us. Many of the people had been coming to the house, bringing Jackie her meals, and would help feed her because I was working.

One day we were looking at a house, left that house and drove around the corner only to see another house with a sign in the yard that had just been put up while we were looking at the previous house. We drove around the block two or three times looking at the house, the lot, the out buildings, the trees and the neighborhood. I decided to pull into the blacktop driveway so we could look at it a little bit better. A young man walked out of the front door and asked if there was anything he could do to help us. It was evident he had been watching these two people in a big pickup "casing" his house. I told him we were just interested in the house, and he asked if we would like to see it. We walked into the house, looked around a little bit, got back into our truck and Jackie said, "This is going to be our home."

We tried to make an offer on the house but they had put it up for auction and did not want to sell it until auction, probably thinking they would get more money for it. We had to arrange for our realtor friend, who was from Columbus to represent us during the auction. He had to register with the auctioneer, and at the same time I had to put a bid on the house. I had no idea what bid to submit so I put a very low dollar offer. It was a surprise to me, but on the day of the auction, the auctioneer started the bidding at the very dollar that I had given him. We were also blessed to have nine people with us in the driveway of the house watching and listening to all that was going on. Our realtor and our banker were there, and they both reminded me that we were only interested in one bid, the last one. While the auction was going on, I happened to turn around to find Jackie and some of the other women in a circle praying. I have been to several auctions and it was a first for me to see people praying. Once it was all over, we bought the house for the very dollar amount that I would have offered them had they accepted a contract a month earlier. At my age I had questioned if I could even get a loan for the house. I want to remind you my banker was there that day, and yes, once again God was faithful, right on time, and never late.

This house was built in about 1952 and it still looked like 1952. The structure of the house was solid, but we wanted to make some changes in it. I want to remind you that earlier I told you Jackie was a great decorator. That day someone suggested we needed to have a wall paper party. After we got possession of the house, on a Friday night, there was a team of people in our house tearing off wallpaper. Once again a paper removing party was new to me, but what a blessing they were. I expanded the bathroom so that it would be more suitable for Jackie, and God would supply many things in those days to help us to fix up our house.

That house was our home longer than any other house we lived in during the nearly forty-seven years of marriage. Jackie was able to live there for six years before becoming a resident of Vancrest nursing home.

Once again we were relegated to be takers. We had always tried to be givers whenever God blessed us to be able to, but now things have changed again. We were once again on the receiving end, and we were being blessed. I'm not sure how many, and I can't recall who, but the help kept coming to assist Jackie both in our home and at Vancrest. However, I know that many of them made the comment that helping Jackie had been a real blessing for them. Even the caretakers at Vancrest said to me many times how she was such a blessing to them. It was proof to me that a person who has a relationship with Christ can be an example no matter in what condition they find themselves. I might have been a little prejudiced, but I didn't solicit their comments. There were times I did get to watch and listen while Jackie talked to some of her caretakers about issues of life and about the need to have Christ in their life. She didn't just talk about life; she also talked about what she received from her personal walk with Christ. I know of one caretaker who was having some real problems, personal problems. She would spend time talking with Jackie, and she would comment about how much that helped her. I want to reemphasize that God will work through anyone who is willing to let Him, no matter what their physical condition may be. Jackie did not always feel like shouting, but she never ceased to give God credit and praise for his blessings.

Some people measure success by how big your house is, or what kind of car or pickup you drive, or where you go on vacation, or what your job title might be. God doesn't consider benchmarks like that as measures of success. He is interested in His most precious creation wanting to spend time with Him. That is why He used someone like Jackie to reach so many people. That is why this love story is not just about two people with a love relationship that grew more solid during difficult times. It is not just about adjustments of personalities to complement each other for a "happy" life, or even just about keeping vows. It is also about God working through someone who was willing to let Him. It is about someone who counted the things of this world as insignificant in the scheme of eternity. It is a story about the love of Christ, how it is displayed through someone who, even in a diseased state, desired to share the good news of hope with others. It is about someone who did not consider herself very important in this world but gave of her love to others when she could barely talk. Jackie would not complain when she was uncomfortable, and still smiled big, giving hugs to anyone who wanted them. Her love for God gave her a desire to be home with Him on a daily basis. I want to reemphasize that when she talked about going home, it was not generic. It was not about going to heaven when I die in the sweet by and by. It was not an attitude that says I will trust God for my trip to heaven, but I want to keep control of everything in my life while here on earth. Jackie's attitude about going to heaven was as if she had seen what God had prepared for us, and she could not wait to go back. It was as if Christ had come in the night, taken Jackie to walk the beautiful shores of the Promised Land, and then told her He would be back tomorrow night for another walk. It was as if He told her, "One of these times, my child, you get to stay there with Me." That is a picture of someone who was successful! God did exactly what He told me He was going to do thirty-two years earlier. He took the disease, Jackie's commitment to serve Him, and gave her the opportunities to share her love for Christ, and used it to minister to others. God blessed. How does He feel when He sees you and what you are doing on a 7/24 basis? He knows exactly what you are feeling and thinking. He knows how you handle your challenges and what your attitude is all the time. Do you want to be successful for eternity or for the few years you are on this earth? Talk to God about what is important to Him. Let Christ show you how to give of yourself and your resources to make others' lives better. Let Him put a love in your heart that is contagious. A disease, a cold, or anything that can be transferred from one person to another, can only be caught from someone who has it. If you are not infectious, you have nothing to catch. Our travels may have been so Jackie could touch, or infect more lives. While God used me in many ways as well, my main mission may have been to facilitate her getting exposed to more people. Our ministry may have been more about Jackie's ministry than mine, and that is okay.

It was very difficult watching Jackie, knowing she could not do much of anything. She could not get up and walk where she wanted. She could not feed herself, and then food became an enemy, not an ally. She could not care for herself, comb her hair, brush her teeth, and sometimes when she was in pain, it was difficult for her to swallow a Tylenol. I could only just sit there and hold her until it quit hurting. There were many things this life did not offer Jackie to be a part of anymore. So it is safe to say she was hurting in some way all the time, physically or emotionally. I don't blame her for wanting to go home, but there is something God showed me through this. When Jackie was having a rough time, it was very difficult for me to watch it happen. How much does it hurt Christ when He has given so much more and we count it as nothing? I would see her every day, every night, good times or bad. Not everyone could see what I was able to see. Life is not always pleasant and I don't always like it. I don't have to like everything to live it. A tragedy can be when a person sacrifices peace in an effort to create happiness for this temporary home instead of preparing for an eternal home.

I remember being a part of a round table discussion we were having in a counseling class after Jackie and I sang for chapel service years ago at Ohio Christian University. It was interesting, as well as educational, listening to comments and having to answer the different questions, concerns, and feelings in that discussion. It was also interesting because it was so impromptu. The heartfelt concerns, the feeling of being uncomfortable while watching us sing. Some wanted to know if singing hurt her, did it hurt her when she got emotional? And some questioned if she should even be trying to sing? The discussion was a delight from the professor's view. He knew the people in this class loved Jackie and me, but some day they may find themselves having issues that would create mixed emotions about something they could or couldn't control. I think everyone at that table was genuinely concerned about Jackie's well-being, but they might find it difficult to be completely honest if it were their fragile emotions. Jackie's ability for ministry had been diminished but had not ceased. Just because her physical body could not tolerate the exertion required, it did not mean her Spiritual Ministry was no longer active. This dreaded disease would have to take her life to keep her from being a witness, and with God's blessing on this book, even death will not stop her witness.

While a disease is not a respecter of persons, God is fully able to work through the person committed to Him, no matter what physical trials they may be experiencing. God wants people who recognize that the physical will remain here while the spiritual will meet Him. A person can enter heaven that is disabled in this life and be healed. A person can choose hell with a perfect physical body, and according to the Bible, be forever in torments. Jackie wanted to go to heaven because she loved Jesus. Was she tired of this world and what she had to live? Sure she was. I am sure of it. I asked her once, "If God would give you the choice of healing you here or taking you home, what would you choose?" She said quickly, "I want to go home." That is a relationship with Christ. That is singing the song and meaning the words. That is not saying how much you look forward to heaven until the opportunity comes and then asking for a little more time. She was ready to go. Given the menu of life, I would not have picked this page of life for us, but you couldn't find enough money to pay for what I learned from it. I learned what it means to trust Him in our personal lives, and in our spiritual lives. We were blessed to have God work in our lives and through our lives for His glory. Watching Jackie made a difference in me as well. We were blessed to be in ministry in so many places in this great country. We were wealthy beyond comprehension with friends. I couldn't go anywhere that I didn't have people genuinely concerned about how Jackie was doing. It was a question that was not just a passing inquiry. They wanted to know. Could God have healed Jackie? I have no doubt that He could.

Let me tell you about a little boy that was just four days from his third birthday when he was in a tragic accident. The family was at the grandparents' farm for the big Fourth of July celebration. There was nothing unusual about that. They were a family that was together a lot in those days. There would be various kinds of fireworks for the celebration, one kind being Roman candles. This little boy was sitting with his uncle, again nothing unusual about that. He spent a lot of time with this uncle but this night would not be a usual celebration. This little boy and his uncle were holding one of the Roman Candles that was supposed to shoot into the air and increase the beauty of this great freedom celebration, but not tonight. The Roman candle did not shoot into the air, but instead it exploded. When it exploded it was right in front of the face of this three-year-old boy. The impact was concentrated on the little boy's face. His grandfather, who was standing above and behind him, was also impacted by the force of the explosion. They quickly took the little boy into the house and tried to wash the charred flesh from his face, but the water rolled off his skin like it was plastic. They put him into the car and drove to the local hospital just two miles down the road only to be told by the hospital, they could do nothing for him there. They were not equipped to handle such a severe burn. The parents again put the boy back into the car of this aunt and uncle and started the 65-mile drive to Children's Hospital in Columbus, Ohio. The Ohio State Highway Patrol met them at the edge of the city and escorted them to the hospital where the medical team was waiting to take him to surgery. The doctors operated for four tedious hours. When surgery was finished, the doctor approached the parents, the aunt, and the uncle to tell them they had done their best but one eye was gone. However, the doctor told them he would be able to see out of one eye a little. The little boy's father would later tell, while walking on the terrace at Children's Hospital praying, two things happened. First, a man approached the father and asked him if he was a Christian, which he was. He told him that his little boy would be in surgery, and asked him to pray for his son, which he did. The second event was when God spoke to this deeply concerned father to remind him that he would be able to see a little out of one eye. The father's response to God was, for both eyes to be the same, one way or the other. The bandages were removed about six days later, and this little boy not only could see, he would not need glasses until he was about 52 years old. He could not only see, he could read the fine print sometimes hidden at the bottom of a contract, as well as look down the road and read a sign before most other people could. God not only healed; He did it right. I know this story well because I am that little boy. I bring this chapter to a close with this story because I want the reader to know that in our house it was never a secret that God could heal my Jackie. She was aware of what God had done for me. Jackie was sitting there when we met the surgeon seventeen years after my accident, and she watched as he shook his head in amazement. She heard him say it was a miracle. Jackie experienced a Divine miracle with our children, but I never one time heard her ask why God didn't heal her of Multiple Sclerosis. She and I both knew God worked in ways we didn't always understand; one way being when He uses someone's illness for ministry when He could have healed them. That is exactly what He had been doing with Jackie. There was not one time she got angry with God because she was sidelined with this disease. There was not one time she questioned His plan for her. Not one time did she raise her hand or fist to God in protest, but many times she raised her hand in praise and thanks to Him.

God can use anyone to reach others when we are willing to say "yes" to Him.

Once, while at a funeral home, I was talking to one of the young ladies that had helped to care for Jackie. A family member had died and there had been a question about whether there was a God or heaven. This young lady said if you want to know if there is a heaven or if God is real, just take a few minutes to talk with Jackie. You will see the evidence of God and heaven.

PS I didn't tell you that the drive from Urbana (65 miles) to Children's Hospital in Columbus after my roman candle accident was on an empty tank of gas. Is anything too great for God? No, there isn't.

CHAPTER 12
Celebration Time

There are special days established each year that we celebrate on a national basis, and some people even get that day off work with pay. There are other days that are only special to certain individuals. We put them on the calendar to highlight that day as something special. Days like birthdays, anniversaries, vacations and more. Jackie was looking for and counting on one particular day. It was not a day that could be marked on the calendar, but a day she knew was coming, and one she was looking forward to. It has been said there are two things for sure, death and taxes. If we pay no more taxes, there still remains the fact we are all going to die. There are those who don't believe there is a heaven to gain and a hell to shun. The fact that we have a free will choice is just that. It is our choice what we believe. I have already stated choices have consequences. I may choose to believe something is false when in fact it is true. I may perceive something to be true when in fact it is not. There can be a big difference between truth and perception of truth. My choice does not change whether something is true or not. My choice does not determine truth or relate to perception. My choice is connected to the consequence of what I believe. Truth is always truth. There are some who want to ignore truth by saying there is no such thing. Let me give you an exercise to establish my point. If you hit your finger with a solid object, it will hurt. No matter how you deny it, that is truth. The evidence is the nerves as they scream in pain! If a person wants to deny the Biblical declaration of a heaven to gain and a hell to shun, they have been given the ability to look the Creator in the eye and say, "I don't believe." That is their choice, but it does not change truth. Jackie believed in Father God's heaven. Her day turned out to be May 28, 2015. That was the day the Father decided it was time for Jackie to come home to be with Him.

Mother's Day was just eighteen days prior to Jackie's victory day. That week was a stressor of a week. It was the week my Stepdad died; I also had to prepare a message for Mother's Day and my Stepdad's memorial service. At the same time, Jackie's heart rate was running over a hundred beats per minute and her oxygen level was in the seventies with two liters of support oxygen being given to her. I was sitting there asking God, "What am I going to do?" My Stepdad had lived out of state, and I was sitting at Jackie's bedside where I wanted to be and should be. I, of course, had no idea what was going to happen with Jackie's condition, and so the question was still "What was I going to do?"

I am so glad I can experience God giving me assurance. I felt like God said to me, "I will give you a reprieve. I will take care of it," and He did. It was just a few minutes later that Jackie's heart rate started to come down and her oxygen level started coming up. By Sunday she was off the oxygen, her heart rate normal, and she was off Hospice critical care. The roller coaster ride just kept getting more interesting all the time.

My sister, Connie, had come from out of state on this Sunday so we could leave Monday morning to drive to Maryland for our Stepdad's memorial service. While she was visiting with Jackie, she was told by Jackie, "When you get back from Maryland, I'm going home." Connie told me about Jackie's statement when she got to my house. I asked if she thought Jackie meant to our house or her heavenly home. She told me Jackie meant her heavenly home. The last several months Jackie would ask me who was going to help me move everything out of her room because she was going home. It was always painful wanting Jackie home with me and knowing that would never happen without God's healing touch.

My sister and I made the trip to Maryland on Monday, had the service on Tuesday and then left to get back home on Wednesday. I called Jackie twice a day while we were gone, but I could tell her voice, conversation, and attitude just seemed different than any time before. We got back too late in the evening Wednesday to visit with Jackie, as she was already asleep. On Thursday morning I went early to see her and help feed her. I had been away for three days and I was anxious to be with her, and see how she was doing. It was not going to be a good day. She could hardly eat. Her ability to swallow had been getting more difficult and that Thursday morning she could only get about three bites of yogurt down. This would be the day, the day after we got home; she started her journey to her heavenly home, just like she said she would. Two weeks later, she got to experience what she had longed for, to be with Jesus and her Heavenly Father. Her last breath here was her first breath in heaven. She fought the fight, finished her course, and kept the faith. I can only imagine what she is seeing now.

CHAPTER 13

The Norm is About to Change

I don't think I ever considered how many times our norm changes until just shortly before Jackie's passing. I was walking down the hall to Jackie's room when my thoughts took me to the many times I had walked this hall in the last several years which was at least once a day. The only day this did not happen was if I had to be out of state, which was seldom. This had become my norm. I did sleep at home, but Jackie's room had become my other home. This is where my wife, my best friend, my love, lived. We had tried to make her room look and feel as much as possible like the family room in our house. Her dad bought her a big screen television. I bought some stand-alone shelves for pictures and other decorative things Jackie liked to look at each day. We had a couch, a lift chair, a rocker, and a straight chair. Sometimes the room was full of visitors and sometimes it was just Jackie and me. The wall was filled with pictures, things the grandkids had made, special items hung where she could see them. Rich, the maintenance supervisor and our friend, was so good to come and hang more wall shelves, pictures and anything else Queen Jackalene wanted (another name I gave her sometimes). She was my Queen and she made me feel like I was her King. So as I was walking down the hall having now realized this was a part of my norm, I also knew the day would come when this norm would change, and I would have to establish a new norm.

It can be interesting, as well as test your patience, when people want to tell you what to expect or that they know how you feel about something when they have never experienced what you are going through. One comment made to me was, however, correct, "You will never be ready." This happened to be correct. I am a detail person, and I try to plan ahead as much as possible. Jackie was much the same way. We would talk about her home going and play the song sung by Mercy Me, "I Can Only Imagine." I was hoping for her sake the Lord would let her go home before me, yet I was not ready for Jackie to leave me. I knew she would be safe and perfect, but I also knew I would miss her.

Jackie touched a lot of lives while she was on this earth. As I reflect on how blessed I was to have her as my wife and partner, it seems like it had been such a short time ago that we were walking down the aisle to give our commitments to each other. We had no idea what was awaiting us in this life, but the one thing we knew-we had God in our life. Life always brings challenges, but I can't imagine what it would have been like to face ours without Christ as our guide. I don't think there is a lot of thought given to future challenges when two people are about to say "I do and I will" to each other. In all the premarital counseling I have done, no one has ever asked the question of how to deal with handicaps and heartaches of this life. The question of pain and testing never comes up. I can't imagine anyone looking forward to a life of wheelchairs and oxygen tanks with excitement. I can say that I have lived a life with a lady that looked at the challenge, trusted in God, left a legacy of not quitting, and continued full steam ahead until there was no more steam. Then she quietly kept her hand in His while He took her home. I would have liked for life to have been a little more normal, but as I have written in this book, there are people who needed to see that being physically challenged does not need to keep us from God's best. God's best is not always wrapped around the ability to perform. It is about Him. The whole idea of this book is to help show life is not just about us. I know there are individuals who struggle with accepting this, but here is a lady who lived it. If anyone had the "right" to say that it wasn't fair, it was Jackie and yet she would answer, "I'm fine."

A new norm would mean never hearing that from her again. It would mean not walking that hall to her room again. It would mean not going in to feed her again.

It would mean never seeing her smile and hearing "hi," in the way only she could say it. Yes, there is a certain relief when someone you love so much has fought the fight and then gets to be eternally safe with Christ. Developing a new norm is a challenge, a challenge that doesn't happen quickly, easily, or comfortably.

Change is a word that can frighten people to do and say things they would otherwise never consider.

I was on a flight once where we had to divert because of weather. The couple next to me seemed pleasant and easy to talk to while in flight. As it became apparent we would be going into a different airport, his mood changed drastically. When the plane landed and we found ourselves trying to get flights to our original destination, I was compelled to feel sorry for the ticket agent. She had no ability to control the weather, and yet she was the one engulfed with people who struggled with change. The amazing sight was that the loudest, most angry person at her counter happened to be the quiet, gentle man who had been sitting next to me in flight. Change is not something that is always pleasant, but how we handle change displays our character.

I am thankful the Father made it possible for me to rest for a while after Jackie passed. I didn't realize how tired my body was. It also gave me time to accept that I didn't need to be everywhere somebody else thought I should be. The popular comment is to stay busy. I had already been busy.

I needed to grieve, rest, and just let Father God minister to me. I would need to be available to my children and grandchildren as much as possible without taking over their lives. I realize not everyone can have the time I was blessed to take. I have said that sometimes we each handle life situations differently. Developing a new norm was something my Father God would have to help me with and will continue to help me. I did not want to crawl into a corner, but neither did I want to wear myself out any more than I already was. I wanted to do it right.

Having someone to talk to is very important, and I was blessed with a very close friend who was a Godsend during this time. I also had a few friends that would call at times to check on me, but there were times when I felt so alone and the phone did not ring. I was now experiencing what others who have suffered with a death have dealt with, and I didn't like it, but that is life. I made the statement that if there was a better way for the life and death experience to happen, God would have done it that way. I have to believe this is the best way, as painful as it is; it is still God's design.

I learned from this experience how blessed I was to have a wife who loved God more than life. I was blessed to have a wife that loved me unconditionally, faithfully, worked by my side with me, prayed for me, and was an example to me and all who knew her. She lived what a Godly wife, mother, daughter, sister, friend is supposed to look like. This was all a part of my last norm with Jackie. Now I must establish a new norm, once again. A new norm with thanks for what God has taught me through the pain of life thus far. Will there be more pain? I imagine.

What will this norm look like? I'm not sure but I know I want to remember what I have learned. I want to make a difference in people's lives by helping them benefit from the pain I have already experienced.

CHAPTER 14

Making Sense Out of Common Sense

According to Dictionary.com, the meaning of "common sense" is "sound practical judgment that is independent of specialized knowledge, training, or the like; normal native intelligence."

I imagine most of us at one time or another have looked at the result of someone's actions and wondered where their common sense was in that decision? If we are willing to be real honest with ourselves, we probably have had more opportunities to look at our own choices than what we like to admit. I am glad I never counted the times in my life where I reflected back on something wondering what made me think that was a good idea. I will say that if we would learn from each time we make a poor decision, we can reduce the need to correct, apologize, or regret having made a bad choice. After all, every choice has a consequence. We can also learn good, helpful ways to repeat opportunities in life from positive decisions.

It is for this reason I have inserted this chapter. My experience has been some people like to be helpful but they don't always know how to accomplish that goal. The fear of intruding into the realm of the unknown with lack of knowledge or experience in a subject, or trying to help a challenged person can be a little scary to an individual, so rather than to appear incompetent and insensitive, some don't even attempt. That choice brings comfort to the fearful person for the moment, but does nothing for future confrontations of the same dilemma, as well as giving no comfort to the person that may have benefited from the contact. They will not have any better idea how to respond to an unknown than before, so a pattern has begun of ignoring, denying interest, or whatever releases them from the possibilities of the issue only to become more of a norm than a choice.

My father was not well most of my life. The medical field did not have the ability to diagnose many of his symptoms as they can today. I watched as my mother would consistently care for Dad when he would come home from work or when we worked on our farm. He had headaches a lot and eventually a brain tumor is what took his life. The key point is that she set before us kids an example that was helpful in making life decisions.

My sister became a very proficient, well-liked and trusted nurse, nursing professor, and then teaching administrator. Her patients would later tell me that she was one of the most caring, dependable nurses they ever had. When she stepped into the teaching arena, I was told that her love for nursing and people went with her in a very infectious way. I was also blessed to visit her in her work environment and witness the respect and appreciation those in her charge had for her. That isn't something you can command, it has to be earned. Once you earn it, it will follow you if you continue to embrace it.

Did the example of our mother caring for our father instigate and nourish this trait or did it come from my sister's personality and God given gifts? I really don't know. I do know that whichever came first was encouraged and given good support by the other.

I tried in the forty-seven years of our marriage to be a good leader to my wife and our two miracle children. In that time and with the development of her disease, one of the decisions I would have to make was do I stay or do I leave? There are too many spouses that don't stay. This is a game changer. Life can no longer be calculated even in our infinite ability to project what comes next. We live in such a "me" society that there are those who would willingly support an exit of responsibility in exchange for selfish thoughts of what they might call a meaningful life. Whatever the basis for preparing me to make a life altering decision, I must also include God as the inspiration in helping me because I never considered leaving. When I said "I will and I do" during the giving of my vows to my bride, I meant it, unconditionally.

I cared for my wife many years and it was during this chapter of our lives I got to see people attempt to be helpful while sometimes not using common sense. It would also be very evident later, after my wife's passing, when I was trying to develop a new norm. The fear of doing something wrong can be such a strain on the heart and mind when we keep God out of the equation.

I remember once a friend asked Jackie how she was doing. We know that often that is a nonrealistic greeting used when a person really doesn't care how you are doing and they certainly don't want you to give them an answer. Jackie replied that she was really tired, which is a normal symptom of MS. Keep in mind, Jackie is sitting in a wheelchair and this person is not. Her answer was, "I know how you feel." Let me break this down a little differently.

1. I, in no way, think this friend had any ill intent. She was genuine in her question. She cared for our family as a whole, but by not being in the same situation as Jackie, she could not relate.

2. If two people are tired, they have weariness in common, but how they got to that point can be totally different. We each one handle situations differently so even if all the elements are the same, we cannot know how someone else feels. If we truly know how they feel, as their friend we don't need to ask them. We already know.

3. This person then, after telling Jackie how tired she was because of all that she has had to do, gets on her feet and walks away.

4. Jackie turned her head to look at me and then I replied to the question on her face, "Just let it go, she means well."

Suggestions:

A. The question is not wrong, just let the person answer you and then drop it if you really don't want more information.

B. If you are concerned and really do want to know, take time to show the compassion you would want them to show to you.

C. Remember, so much of the time we consciously or unconsciously think life is just about us.

Another careless statement often made, "Let me know if there is something I can do." Yes, I have some suggestions for this one! You knew I would. I will personalize again to illustrate.

You are looking at a lady in a wheelchair who used to keep a spotless house, take care of two children (three if you count me), be a great cook, and still resemble what Eve must have looked like.

- Do you think there is a need there?

- Do you think you have to ask?

- Do you think she or I will ask you to come to our house to cook a meal and clean our toilets? I don't think so.

Here are some thoughts. Don't ask a question you know is not genuine.

1. The statement, "If I can do anything," appears that you really don't want to sacrifice your time and effort outside of your own world. Making a difference is about action and not empty words.

2. If you really are not able to help in this hour of distress, and that can be reality, just give some special attention to the hurting person at that moment without comments that suggest something you know you are not going to fulfill.

3. Don't make an offer out of guilt if you are not able to fulfill your commitments because it brings more pain to someone in need.

4. If you are able to help, understand and accept you don't have to do it all.
   a. Set a time limit that you can be available to help.

    b. Bring someone with you. Two people can get more done in the same time, but make sure it is someone you would want to help you in your home or property.

    c. Bring someone else with you that can sit and visit with the person you are helping. It is often assumed that some people get many visitors, but that is not always the case. Be courteous and ask ahead of time, especially if you are bringing someone unfamiliar.

    d. Ask if you can bring a group.

        1. Ladies might enjoy getting a lot accomplished that they can't do for themselves, and the extra company might be very uplifting.

        2. Men might like having some help with things they just can't do anymore. It might be nice to take an extra lawn chair along just to sit and tell stories for a bit.

5. Consider the person in need and ask yourself, "What do I think I would feel like, if I were in their condition?" There is no way you can understand unless you have been in their position, and then remember, we all handle things differently. Even if you think you know how they are feeling, let them express it to you.

6. I believe there are people who want to be helpful but they are afraid of saying something wrong, sounding uninformed, insensitive, or they are just scared.

    a. Being a good friend is not about being perfect in all things. It is about being.

    b. We are such a doer society that we fail to realize the greatest asset is being.

    c. *Let your light so shine before men, that they may see your good works and glorify your Father in Heaven* (Matthew 5:16 NKJV). Glorify the Father, not ourselves, is something some struggle with because they want to look good in the sight of others.

    d. Being, keeps the focus on the Father, glorifying Him because He has put the light within us. That is why we can shine. A light bulb can look great and appear ready to glow but without the power it produces nothing.

    e. It is not about us. To be a good friend to someone in need is to make yourself available to them by being there. This minimizes the fear of doing the wrong thing so you can be what they most need, which is not being alone.

7. Many have quoted this, "People don't care how much you know until they know how much you care". I watched Jackie as caring people would

come and spend time with her. I could tell by the expression on her face how much it meant to her to have people who cared and shared their gift of time with her. Sometimes they would have to carry both sides of the conversation, or read to her, or just sit there, but she knew they cared. They gave what they could never get back, their time. That is being.

8. Take some people with you and sing to people who are shut-in. We had a church that would come with people of all ages including children to Vancrest. They were good singers, but more importantly, they were a blessing. Jackie would lie there with a big smile on her face, and when she could, raise her hand to acknowledge she knew who they were singing about.

9. Ask questions:
    a. Can we bring something to eat? What do you like? Make sure they are allowed to have whatever you bring to them.
    b. Would you like me to read to you?
    c. Would you like to watch a movie or listen to a CD?
    d. Do you like board games? Make sure they are able to play them.
    e. Be observant. Pay attention, by doing so you may notice other ways you can help.

10. You may learn that some things are best left unsaid and that is okay. Give these suggestions a try and while you are trying, listen to yourself.

11. Take some younger people with you to be a blessing to the home bound or nursing-home bound. The youth will get a new perspective and many more benefits. Remember, someday it may be you waiting for visitors.

12. Be able to listen without always having to offer solutions. If a person is not able to participate in normal activities of life, they might need someone to talk to, someone who will keep the conversation confidential. They may just need to vent or cry away the pain. They may need someone they feel they can trust. Having someone to talk to who will listen, will not judge, will not feel a need to fix it, is willing to put their arm around them while they cry, and will express genuine Godly love, is rare. Are you one of those people?

13. Don't be surprised if you come to encourage, and leave changed yourselves.

14. Remember the golden rule: be to other people what you would like for them to be to you. It's not that hard.

CONCLUSION

My hope and prayer has been that God could use this book to make a difference in someone's life. My emotions have varied much like a roller coaster ride as I have been writing. This is not something I am doing from my comfort zone, but I have felt it was a project the Lord led me to do. According to my research, there are roughly sixty-five million people in the United States that are considered handicapped or disabled. My hope is that someone will read this book and see by Jackie's example that they are loved. I want them to realize they have value. I want people with challenges to have the confidence to use the gifts God has given them.

My hope is that caretakers will read this book and realize they are not alone. The feelings that we experience are real. Life is real, and it is not always what we might have expected when we said "I do," but it can be rewarding when we consider the needs of our loved one ahead of ourselves. There are times when we have frustrations and pain that don't seem to let up. Our task is to consider the pain of the precious person who looks to us to keep some stability and normalcy in their challenged life. Sometimes we are too quick to try and find someone or something to blame for the challenges that have come our way. Were there times when I was tired and felt like nothing was going the way it should? There were. Did those times bring a host of other emotions? They did. Were there times when I didn't handle situations correctly? You can believe that, too. Were there times when I had to apologize for my attitude? More often than I like to think about it.

This is not a book about how to be perfect, or handle complications without error. It is written to be a book about how God can make a difference in any situation if given the opportunity. The difficulties of life are in this world, but not for eternity if we have accepted Christ as our personal Savior. Every choice has a consequence. If it is a good choice, it can have a good consequence. If it is a bad choice, it can have a bad consequence. Did I ever consider leaving my wife and children because it was too tough? Not once. Would I have liked for it to be different? Of course I would. Did it help to see God working in the whole situation? It was a blessing to know someone was being helped. Did I think about how disease would not be known in heaven? I thought of that on a regular basis. What was my most stabilizing, comforting, consistent, assuring, genuine support? Father God. I don't know what I would have been without Him.

You may be facing what you just read about in this book or know someone who is. Don't give up on God, and remember God loves you.

A Final Tribute to a Christian Lady

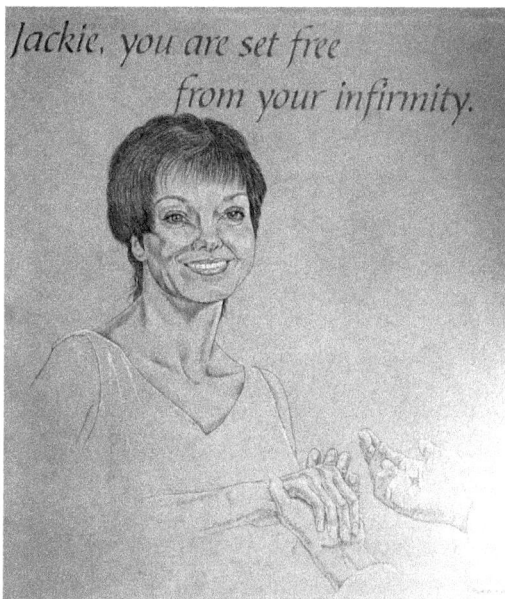

Jackie, you are set free from your infirmity.

Born August 19, 1950
Home May 28, 2015

So rest, my dear, in the beautiful hands of Jesus. You have finished your race of obstacles and challenges, and you did it well. You sacrificed going to college to work and help me continue my studies. You endured and rose above the accusations from gossiping co-workers. You successfully endured unkind remarks that brought many tears but not defeat. You won the battle of near death in child birth. You had to ignore some comments that hurt while still learning to be a good pastor's wife. You still had the fortitude at such a young age to become a great example of the lady of the parsonage and mother. You never complained, but instead you were very supportive when God led us to move eighteen times. You went from house to house leaving it better than when we arrived, while knowing it would never belong to you. Little did we know each of the moves we made was designed by God for His purpose. You went back to work at times when we needed some extra income, but you continued to organize and orchestrate the house while working a full time job. You were willing to move four hours away from family in our first pastorate. You were also willing later to move two thousand miles away from family because God asked you to do it. When life brought to you a disease that you could not get rid of and I could not fix, we turned it over to the Lord. You never blamed Him for it even when you could not talk straight or see well. There were times when you could no longer walk, or stand, without help. I wondered if it was enough for you to know that you were an example of suffering for Jesus. The night you asked me to pray that you could stand alone to raise your hands the next day when we sang the part, "Oh, for a thousand hands to raise," in the song, "Oh For a Thousand Tongues to Sing," by David Binion, what a blessing! When my hand or my arm was not enough support, and you required a walker, still the smile of Jesus was on your face. When a walker was no longer sufficient, you didn't complain when we had to use a wheelchair. When you could no longer feed yourself, you adapted to that with a smile, as well. When I had to get help to care for you, to feed you, to bathe you, to stay with you every hour until I got home, you endured your loss of privacy with a Christ-like attitude. When you had to drink through a straw and yogurt became your friend, again a smile. The weeks we spent in the hospital, you were the best patient they had. There were the periods of pain that was evident when it took your smile, but it couldn't have your victory because of your love for Christ. The four years and six months that you spent in a care facility, you still were an example of Christ in word and action. The many times you wanted to go to be with Jesus but had to wait until God's timing was complete, you did it with a smile. All this and more because there is no way of describing the looks, the glances, the eyes, all the expressions that are included in the personality of love Christ can put in our hearts for Him. There is, however, one expression that can bring this tribute to a partial close. When asked the question, "How are you doing, Jackie?" You would answer, "I'm fine."

About the Author

Tom Amlin was born and raised in Ohio, living on a farm until he graduated from high school and attended Urbana University. His ambition was to become a basketball coach and math teacher. That changed after visiting Circleville Bible College, now known as Ohio Christian University, where he later received his degree in ministry and counseling. His visit there was to be a fun weekend with friends, but while there, God brought conviction on his life. Tom committed his life to Christ that weekend and met Jackie Small who would become his bride just fourteen months later.

Tom and Jackie served together in the pastorate, music ministry, youth camp ministry, evangelism, staff ministry, teaching and missions. Tom has been a licensed minister over fifty years and faced many life experiences. The driving force of his obedience to serve in ministry has been his love for God and people. He has a goal to use his gifts and experiences to help people through the pain of life. One of Tom's favorite Bible verses reads,

Isaiah 41:10 "Fear thou not for I am with thee: be not dismayed; for I am thy God: I will strengthen thee; yea, I will help thee; yea, I will uphold thee with the right hand of my righteousness".

www.beautifulhandsministries.com
email: beautifulhandsministries@gmail.com

www.ingramcontent.com/pod-product-compliance
Lightning Source LLC
LaVergne TN
LVHW051103080426
835508LV00019B/2031